Lean Applications in Sales

Lean Applications in Sales

How a Sales Manager Applied Lean Tools to Sales Processes and Exceeded His Goals

Jaideep Motwani and Rob Ptacek

First published in 2014 by
Business Expert Press, LLC
222 East 46th Street, New York, NY 10017
www.businessexpertpress.com

ISBN-13: 978-1-60649-766-1 (paperback)
ISBN-13: 978-1-60649-767-8 (e-book)

Business Expert Press Selling and Sales Force Management Collection

Collection ISSN: 2161-8909 (print)
Collection ISSN: 2161-8917 (electronic)

Cover and interior design by Exeter Premedia Services Private Ltd, Chennai, India

First edition: 2014

10 9 8 7 6 5 4 3 2 1

Printed in the United States of America.

Abstract

Over the past decade Lean methods and tools have helped manufacturing organizations improve their productivity levels significantly by focusing on data, systematic elimination of waste, and improvement of flow. Today many nonmanufacturing organizations are applying the powerful process improvement methods and tools employed with Lean techniques. Organizations in health care, education, government, hospitality, and other services are applying the improvement tools with growing levels of success.

Sales people around the world have watched their organizations improve their core value-added processes, and yet they have not fully engaged or embraced the use of Lean tools in their sales processes. In fact, we've heard several disturbing comments from sales teams such as "Lean won't work in our area, we're too dynamic." And "Six Sigma analyses will just slow us down; we work more on sales instincts here."

While these comments are believed to be true by some sales teams, other sales teams that have used the Lean methods and tools are finding significant improvement opportunities, and they believe that if their "instincts" were good, before the application of these tools, they are even better after the application.

Lean tools are in their most basic sense process improvement tools. Dr. Deming indicated that if one's work cannot be defined as a process, there can be no standardization, and the resultant variation in outcomes will be unacceptable. Sales and sales management are simply a series of processes, which once defined can be continually improved with the application of Lean methods and tools to eliminate wastes and improve flow and speed. While it is true that many sales processes involve the "human element" and relationship building in customer decision making, process improvement tools will help make a good sales person or team better.

This book illustrates lean methods and tools applications applied to a full range of sales organizations and processes. By covering these tools in various sales environments in a story book format, sales team leaders can begin to understand how these methods and tools can be applied in their organizations. Through a unique and easy reading story of a frustrated sales team leader, discovering the power of these tools, the authors present a compelling argument to begin using Lean in sales organizations. This story illustrates the discovery, application, and transformation of sales processes.

Sales managers and sales team leaders will benefit from this book by developing a clear understanding of why and how improvement tools such as Lean can be used to improve their organizations. The authors demonstrate in this book how key components of Lean apply to sales organizations and processes. The authors demonstrate how the proper use of these simple and effective tools can drive sales organizations continuing efforts to identify and reduce waste, improve performance, and speed delivery.

Keywords

continuous improvement, Lean, Lean Sigma, sales, sales management, Six Sigma, waste elimination

Contents

CHAPTER 1

The Lean Sigma for Sales Challenge

"I can't believe it, another lost sale! That's the third one this month! This never used to happen," whined Bill, the sales manager at Rapid Products.

"Never?" replied Sam, the purchasing manager at Rapid Products.

"Well, almost never," said Bill.

"Do you even know what your proposal success rate is?" injected Sam.

"Well, not really; we never really tracked it," replied Bill.

"Now that 'never' I can believe," said Sam.

"We never had to; we used to get almost ever proposal we provided, and now we seem to be losing more than we win," explained Bill.

"Never and almost; it sounds like you don't have a clue what you win or lose and why. It's a wonder that we even stay in business. What's your process for closing a deal?" asked Sam.

"Process?" inquired Bill.

"Yeah, process—what are the steps your sales people use to close a deal?" asked Sam.

"We don't use a *process*. Processes are for our manufacturing group, with their work instructions and procedures and such. Sales is different; there is no standard sales process for sales. We have to build relationships with potential customers and do our magic to close the deal," explained Bill.

"Magic? Now I understand the problem, let's grab lunch and talk a bit," said Sam. Bill shook his head in submission and agreed to lunch.

Rapid Products is a manufacturer of blenders and other small kitchen appliances for Lean Chef, a global firm specializing in small kitchen and cooking appliances. Rapid Products is vertically integrated in that they not only assemble the products—such as blenders, choppers, and knife sharpeners—but they also produce most of the metal and plastic components that make up the units. Rapid Products operates metal stamping and plastic molding presses and associated cleaning and processing equipment for parts produced on these machines.

Rapid Products produces three models of blenders in various colors for each model of blender. A summary of the models and colors is shown subsequently.

The following blender models are produced:

- Master Lean: This is a high-end blender designed for commercial applications that comes with a black, silver, or white base.
- Lean Chef: This is the signature mid-level line designed for serious at-home cooks; it has fewer features and a slightly less powerful motor than the Master Chef model. This model comes with a white, red, or tan color base.
- Gemba Chef: The Gemba Chef model is an entry-level blender designed for a low consumer price point. It has only basic features and a smaller motor than other models, and comes with a black or white base.

Blender assemblies include metal components, plastic molded components, electrical subassemblies, and purchased motor, packaging materials, and various fasteners and lubricants.

The Rapid Products plant is a large sprawling plant with more than 500 square feet under one roof. They are traditionally organized by department or function. The plastic molding machines and tool storage is in a contained area at the north end of the building. The metal stamping and finishing is near the south end of the facility, with certain specialty areas, such as cleaning and subprocessing, located in isolated areas throughout the plant. As Rapid Products grew, they were forced to put equipment where they had space. They have work-in-process (WIP) inventory scattered near work centers throughout the plant as well. Assembly and subassembly lines are centrally located, not too far from the 12 shipping and receiving docks. Their finished goods (FG) inventory is located in a random rack storage area near the docks, and their shipping personnel pick and ship to the daily schedule and hot list every day.

From a scheduling aspect, Rapid Products receives weekly pulls from their large retail customers, as well as small orders from other retailers and distribution centers. Rapid Products must ensure orders are shipped by the end of the following week.

Rapid Products's primary sales markets are major and minor retailers and distributors. They have also recently established an online product line intended to fill a direct sale market void. The sales team regularly provides quotations and proposals for new and existing products to new and existing customers. The proposals and quotations provided by the Rapid Products sales teams vary in that they may or may not include provisions for inventory commitments, volume incentives, deliver commitments, multiple or single lines, special packaging and private labeling, as well as other options dreamed up by creative purchasing managers.

Recently, Rapid Products has been losing sales, and the conversation between Sam and Bill begins to shed some light onto the mystery.

At lunch Bill and Sam continued to discuss the declining sales issue and the need for a sales process.

"So why do I need a sale process?" asked Bill. "We used to do just fine with our relationship approach."

"Well the relationship approach still is important, but today consumers and buyers are much better informed and have so much more information at their fingertips that sales people must provide even better information, faster and with reliable consistency so that informed potential customers can expect and plan on the outcomes of the proposal. In other words, there needs to be a consistent sales process that buyers can count on every time, with no mistakes, no hidden costs, and no surprises. For example, in the old days when we were planning a new contract for electrical motors we used to request a quote from four or five potential suppliers. They'd take us to lunch and wine and dine the buyer to try to get key information on buying preferences and price points. After that process, we'd typically buy the motors from the supplier with the lowest quoted price. The sales person with the better relationship may or may not get better information from the buyer. Now we consider only the top two or three prequalified suppliers, and we establish the price targets for them. The potential suppliers either accept the price targets or not, and then must demonstrate the features, advantages, and benefits of working with them versus their competition. Their profit comes from their ability to lower their internal costs, not in how well they negotiate prices or how great their relationship is with the buyer. In fact, the last electrical motor contract we committed to, we worked together with the supplier to lower our overall total costs, and agreed to share the cost savings equally. The total cost includes the delivery, errors, rework, rejections, inspection and testing costs, and many more hidden costs that did not show up on the unit price. We worked with the supplier on streamlining the supply chain and inspection plans, and actually paid a higher unit price in exchange for other savings. In the final analysis, the actual landed cost of the motors was way below the per unit price. We were able to get to this point not by relationship, but by sales process," lectured Bill.

"Yeah, yeah, yeah—I get it, we do some of that too, but I'm still not sure why we are losing sales lately," interrupted Sam.

"Well what does your lost sales data say is the issue?" asked Sam.

"My what?" replied Bill.

"Your lost sales data. Lost sales data is the assignable cause for losing the sale. Do you even know why your potential customers are going with another supplier?" asked Sam.

"Not really, after we lose a sale, we just get busy trying to get the next one," replied Bill.

"I'll tell you what, we are having a Supplier Day next week and I'd like you to attend. We will be covering Lean and Six Sigma expectations for our key suppliers, as well as our expectations regarding our supplier's sales process outcomes. I think you could learn a lot from the sessions," offered Sam.

"I can make it any day except Thursday. I'm golfing with our largest customer on Thursday," said Bill with a smile.

"I hope he doesn't tell you he's pulling the business!" joked Sam. "You pick up the lunch tab, and I'll plan to see you next week."

"Deal," replied Bill.

Discussion Questions

1. Why did Bill, the sales manager of Rapid Products, agree to have lunch with Sam, the purchasing manager? Do you think Sam could help Bill to better understand the sales process?

2. Do you agree with Bill's statement, "We used to do fine with our relationship approach." Isn't sales about relationship building? How would you convince Bill or other salespeople in your organization about the need for streamlining the sales process?

3. What do you think about Sam's explanation to Bill regarding the need for the sales process in addition to relationship building?

4. Does your organization keep track of lost sales? Do you think it is important to do so? Why or why not?

CHAPTER 2

Identification and Understanding of Lean Sigma

"Okay Sam, where do you want me to sit?" asked Bill.

"You'd better sit right up front Bill, I don't want you to miss anything," replied Sam.

The Supplier Day group consisted of the top 15 suppliers to Rapid Products, and the materials from the session were to be published and placed online for the remaining Rapid Products suppliers. The agenda for the Supplier Day event is as follows:

1. Welcome and interactive introductions.
2. Rapid Products company business outlook.
3. Rapid Products company supplier expectations.
   a. Lean
   b. Six Sigma
   c. Sales process expectations
   d. Improvement sharing
4. Lunch with Rapid Products executive team.
5. Contract reviews.
6. Questions and answers.
7. Closure.

Bill was a bit embarrassed as he introduced himself to the group. He felt that as the SM of Rapid Products he should already know this stuff, and that he was the customer in the room. Soon Bill became humbled by the discussions.

Not only did Sam's purchasing group describe the business conditions in detail, Bill thought that they also had a better perspective on future business than he did as SM. Bill felt too that the purchasing group shared some fairly sensitive information with the suppliers, information that took him months to gain from his potential customers with his relationship selling techniques. Bill took notes and planned to discuss this with Sam later.

As the Lean and Six Sigma discussion was held, Bill took the following notes:

1. Six Sigma and Lean, sometimes called *Lean Sigma* is the most successful continuous improvement methods in the world's history.
2. Lean Sigma combines the simple and versatile methods and tools of Lean with the powerful analytical approach of Six Sigma methods to provide continuous incremental improvement with Lean, and significant increases in productivity and quality with Six Sigma techniques.
3. Lean Sigma is the combination of these powerful tools.
4. The origin of these methods goes back to the industrial revolution and the concept of time and motion studies with Fredrick Taylor and Henry Ford's production lines. Lean Sigma represents the philosophy of total conservation of resources.
5. Edwards Deming brought this to Japan after World War II, and is credited with Lean Sigma's predecessor, Total Quality Management (TQM), which focuses on the customers' needs, continuous improvement, and employee involvement.
6. Dr. Deming worked with Toyota Motor Company, Motorola, and others to implement his TQM systems, and develop the methods and tools we now know as Lean Sigma. Often the Toyota production system, waste elimination, and process or continuous improvement are used synonymously with Lean Sigma methods throughout the world.

Bill knew that the production group at Rapid Products was using the Lean Sigma improvement methods and tools, yet he had never attended an improvement session or event. Bill thought to himself how great this was for manufacturing, but he wasn't convinced it worked in sales. Bill continued to take notes.

What Is Lean, Six Sigma, and Lean Sigma?

Lean is a way of thinking and can be applied to every type of organization, whether it manufactures a product or delivers a service. Lean methods and tools are simple to learn and apply, and have broad applications. Lean methods even work in people's personal lives! People can apply Lean tools to their hobbies, chores, and households to make things simpler, easier, and more enjoyable and cost-effective. The goal of lean is to strive for perfection by minimizing and ultimately eliminating waste, which causes variation throughout the value stream. *The entire focus of lean is customer-driven and it's the customer who determines the value and the amount he or she is willing to pay for the product or service.* The customer enjoys the fruits of the information and material flow. Information and material flows are often documented in Value Stream Maps as shown in the following.

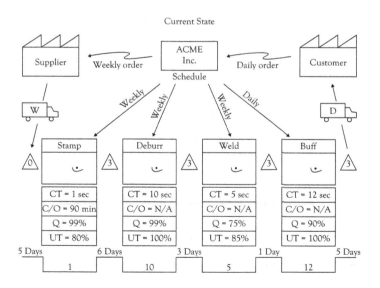

or

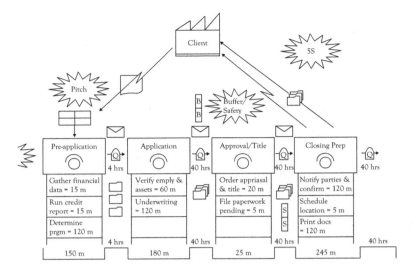

Source: Ptacek and Motwani.

Like Lean, Six Sigma, or 6σ, is another approach that an organization can implement to achieve excellence. Six Sigma is a statistical term. Sigma (σ) defines the variation or "spread" of a process. Six Sigma defines how much of the total process falls within the normal process variation.

The term *Six Sigma* refers to the number of standard deviations away from the mean in a bell-shaped normal distribution curve (see subsequently).

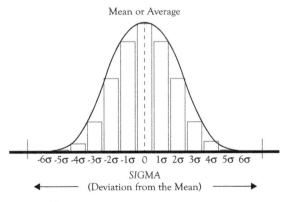

The goal of Six Sigma is to eliminate defects and minimize variability. In statistical terms, if an organization achieves Six Sigma level of performance, 99.99966 percent of its customers are satisfied as they are receiving services that are defect-free and meet their expectations. In other words, an organization that has achieved Six Sigma status will have no more than 3.4 complaints, defects, or errors per million opportunities. The following table summarizes sigma or variation level and error rate per million opportunities.

Process capability or sigma level	Defects (or errors) per million opportunities (DPMO)	Percent acceptable
6σ	3.4	99.99966%
5σ	233	99.9767%
4σ	6,210	99.379%
3σ	66,807	93.32%
2σ	308,538	69.15%
1σ	691,462	30.9%

Six Sigma forces organizations to pursue perfection by asking if 99 percent acceptability is good enough. If 99 percent acceptable is good enough, consider the following:

99% Good (3.8 Sigma)	99.99966% Good (6 Sigma)
20,000 lost articles of mail per hour (based on 2,000,000/h)	Seven lost articles per hour
Unsafe drinking water for almost 15 minutes each day	One unsafe minute every seven months
5,000 incorrect surgical operations per week	1.7 incorrect operations per week
Two short or long landings daily at an airport with 200 flights/day	One short or long landing every five years
2,000,000 wrong drug prescriptions each year	680 wrong prescriptions per year
No electricity for almost seven hours each month	One hour without electricity every 34 years

Lean Sigma is the most powerful improvement technique as it systematically blends the best of the two earlier approaches to eliminate all waste or nonvalue-added activities from processes. This, in turn, lowers the cost and improves the quality of the process. The continued focus on the elimination of waste should be a daily, hourly, or minute-by-minute concern. Lean Sigma is designed to use people and materials wisely to satisfy customer needs. With that thought in mind, work elements or job duties may need to be modified to accommodate a waste-free Lean Sigma environment. This will allow companies to remain globally competitive, develop a cross-trained workforce, and establish a safe workplace.

Lean Sigma tools are used to

- improve customer satisfaction and total customer experience;
- identify and eliminate waste quickly and efficiently;
- increase communication and speed at all levels of the organization;
- reduce costs, improve quality, and meet delivery obligations of a product or service in a safe environment;
- initiate improvement activities and empower employees to make improvements themselves;
- track and monitor improvements to ensure sustainability.

Lean Sigma is truly a compilation of world-class continuous improvement practices.

To understand Lean Sigma, one must understand that Lean Sigma is, in its broadest sense, *a philosophy of conservation of resources and waste elimination*. Building on the Lean Sigma philosophy are Lean Sigma principles, concepts, methods, and tools. These ideas are building blocks of a structured and supported approach to a total Lean Sigma transformation. Lean Sigma principles must be built on a basic understanding of Lean Sigma philosophy. Many organizations have forgone a basic understanding of Lean Sigma philosophy, and tried to build a Lean Sigma organization on a weak foundation, only to be disappointed with their results. It truly pays to start with, and builds on a strong foundation of Lean Sigma understanding.

Conceptually, these building blocks are illustrated in the following diagram. Starting with a strong foundation of Lean Sigma philosophy, Lean Sigma principles can be used to support an organization in utilizing Lean Sigma concepts, methods, and tools, to become a superior organization.

Bill was starting to understand his role as a leader, and continued to listen to the training materials from the Rapid Products Supplier Day.

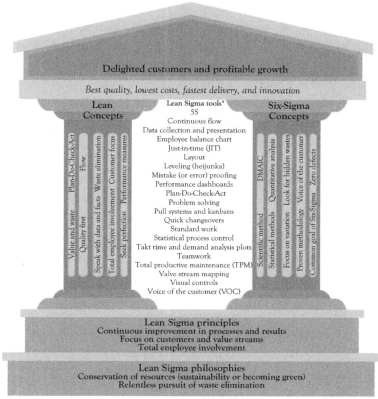

Delighted customers and profitable growth

Best quality, lowest costs, fastest delivery, and innovation

Lean Concepts

Lean Sigma tools*
5S
Continuous flow
Data collection and presentation
Employee balance chart
Just-in-time (JIT)
Layout
Leveling (heijunka)
Mistake (or error) proofing
Performance dashboards
Plan-Do-Check-Act
Problem solving
Pull systems and kanbans
Quick changeovers
Standard work
Statistical process control
Takt time and demand analysis plots
Teamwork
Total productive maintenance (TPM)
Valve stream mapping
Visual controls
Voice of the customer (VOC)

Six-Sigma Concepts

Plan-Do-Check-Act · Flow · Speak with data and facts · Waste elimination · Total employee involvement · Customer focus · Seek perfection · Performance measures

Value and waste · Quality first

DMAIC · Scientific method · Statistical methods · Quantitative analysis · Focus on variation · Look for hidden wastes · Proven methodology · Voice of the customer · Common goal of Six-Sigma · Zero defects

Lean Sigma principles
Continuous improvement in processes and results
Focus on customers and value streams
Total employee involvement

Lean Sigma philosophies
Conservation of resources (sustainability or becoming green)
Relentless pursuit of waste elimination

* Not all inclusive of Lean Sigma tools

Source: Ptacek and Motwani, *Pursuing Perfect Service.*

While on break, Bill took a closer look at each of the Lean Sigma building block levels shown subsequently.

Bill's notes on the building blocks are as follows.

Lean Sigma Philosophies and Principles

The overriding philosophy of Lean Sigma is defined by the continuous elimination of waste and nonvalue-added activities in everything we do, the conservation of all resources at every level of operation. Additionally, Lean Sigma philosophies include continuous learning and improvement in everything that's done. Lean Sigma philosophy calls for the simplification of all tasks and efforts to eliminate waste and improve flow. Absolute perfection is seen as the goal. Very few organizations embrace Lean Sigma philosophies at this level. Toyota Motor Company has been practicing Lean Sigma for over 60 years, and they still believe they need to improve!

Lean Sigma principles are the bedrock for Lean Sigma transformations. They provide the unchanging, solid foundation to build and improve upon. The three key Lean Sigma principles, supported by Lean Sigma philosophies are as follows:

- *Continuous improvement in processes and results*: Do not be "results or bottom-line only" focused. Instead, focus on processes that deliver consistent, waste-free results.
- *Focus on customers and value streams*: Focus on the entire process, from the customer pull or demand to demand fulfillment and customer satisfaction. Focus on how materials and information flow through a process.
- *Employee participation in a nonblaming—fear-free environment*: Organization leaders must make it safe for people to suggest possible improvements in the way things are done.

Lean Sigma Concepts

Lean Sigma concepts drive Lean Sigma transformations. It is essential that people at all levels be trained in and understand Lean Sigma concepts to facilitate a smooth and effective Lean Sigma transformation. Do not underestimate the power of these concepts.

Bill knew he had a lot of training and communication to do if he wanted his sales teams to apply Lean Sigma methods and tools, and continued to take the following notes.

The Lean Sigma concepts are as follows:
- Add value and remove waste
  Value added
  Organizations add value when they change the weight, shape, configuration, properties, or attributes of materials or information. These are the things the customer is willing to pay for.

Waste (nonvalue-added)

Waste is anything that does not add value. Nonvalue-adding activities fall into the 12 categories of waste. Things that consume time, resources, or space, or both but do not contribute to satisfying customer need.

The 12 categories of waste are as follows:

1. Over production: making more than is needed
2. Expertise: not using people's knowledge
3. Transportation
4. Inventory and work in process (WIP)
5. Motion
6. Rework or corrections
7. Over processing: processing more than is needed
8. Waiting or delays
9. Overload or straining a system: overloading systems capabilities, usually leads to other forms of waste
10. Unevenness: unevenness in work flow usually lead to other wastes
11. Environmental waste: pollution, excess consumption
12. Social waste: social networking while at work, literacy, hunger, or cultural oppression

Bill wondered why "time" was not a waste. He concluded that each of the 12 wastes waste time as well! He continued to take notes on Lean concepts.

- Plan, do, check, act (PDCA) process for implementing improvements. This process mirrors the scientific method and drives improvement activities.
- Next process or operation is the customer: serve them.
- Upstream quality: build quality in; do not "pass along" poor quality.
- Customer needs first: always focus on the customers and their requirements.
- Decisions at the lowest appropriate level: go to where the work is done or the value is added. It is sometimes called "Gemba."

- Speak with data: use objective information to evaluate process performance. Use other statistical tools to turn subjective information into objective data.
- Variation reduction and control through statistical process control.
- Define and seek perfection.

Adding value through waste identification and elimination is a fundamental concept of Lean Sigma. The customer is paying for value; waste is anything that your organization does to a product or a service for which the customer may be paying, and probably should not be. Waste is anything that adds time, resources, or cost without adding value to the finished product or service. When waste is removed value increases. Waste can occur in customer processes as well.

Finally, the expected outcomes of Lean Sigma initiatives were covered for the Supplier Day attendees. The list was very impressive, and Bill wondered how this could work in a sales area. Bill's notes are shown in the following.

Lean Sigma Outcomes

Successful Lean Sigma transformations have been documented for hundreds of enterprises in nearly all sectors of the economy. In planning your Lean Sigma transformation, be careful not to set your expectations too low. Organizations implementing Lean Sigma transformations can expect to realize some or all of the following.

- High organization morale, teamwork, and effort through alignment of goals and measures, and improved leadership.
- Clear communication of priorities, expectations, and results through visual and statistical controls. The "right" things get done "right."
- Clean, organized, and efficient worksite: minimal waste or errors.
- High-quality outputs and results.
- Smooth flow of work or services.

- No unscheduled downtime or surprises.
- Perfection: Zero defects or errors.
- Less inventory, delays, transportation, motion, and rework.
- Less costs, more profit, and return on investment.
- Increased capacity, and sales growth potential.

All of this information was a bit overwhelming for Bill. He still wasn't convinced that Lean Sigma would work for a sales organization, but he didn't have many alternatives. He knew that doing the same thing and expecting different results would just not work!

He was looking forward to the sales process discussion after the break. At break Bill made a bee-line for Sam.

"How could you share such sensitive information with our suppliers?" asked Bill through pursed lips.

"Sensitive information; what sensitive information?" replied Sam.

"You told everyone our sales goals, what markets we were targeting, and even the problems we're having breaking into new markets. Why'd you have to share our dirty laundry?" whined Bill.

"Bill, we want our suppliers to team up with us for success. We want them to know the good, the bad, and the ugly. We challenge them to help us achieve our goals. To get their help, we need them to know where we are going and what our key issues are. There is no sense in keeping them in the dark. We need their help to succeed," retorted Sam. "In fact next week we'll be running a joint Lean Sigma even with a supplier. That's where we really share our dirty laundry, maybe you should attend that session to get a better understanding of what we expect from our suppliers," continued Sam.

"I can't make it; I'll be busy making sales calls to follow-up on the quotes I put out this week. I don't think I need it anyway, I see what you're doing here. I think I'll stay for the sales process expectations that's next, but then I should go, I probably have 50 requests for quotes in my email!" said Bill.

"That's your call Bill, but I think you could use it. I think your entire team would benefit," said Sam.

"Now I know you've lost it; there's no way my whole team could attend, we're way too busy," replied Bill.

"If you say so it must be true. We'd better get back to our seats, the session is about to start," said Sam.

"I'll catch up to you later." Bill said as they walked back to their seats.

Sale Process Expectations

Bill was shocked at the requirements Rapid Products had for the sales teams of their suppliers. The requirements read like a quality manual, with the supplier "shall" have this, and the supplier "should" have that, and so on. Bill wasn't sure he could be a supplier to his own company!

First and foremost, the expectation was that each supplier shall have a defined and documented sales process. This could be in any form, but had to be clearly defined with metrics to indicate performance and success levels. It was explained that the sales process definition document should include the inputs required, the supplier of the inputs, the process to construct the cost estimate and quote, as well as the outputs and output applications and users.

It was preferable that the sales process start at opportunity identification, and end with product and or first article delivery. It was also preferred that the first article approval process be clearly defined, and Rapid Products shared their internal first article approval process in effort to show an example. Rapid Products's first article approval process is shown as follows:

1. Produce product to specifications.
2. Obtain engineering and quality files from intranet.
3. Obtain product and all associated parts.
4. Complete product or part dimensional layout per customer drawing if available, or RP print, documenting all dimensions on worksheet according to WI32-765.
5. Complete RP's First Article Submission form per WI32-767.
6. Complete customer First Article Submission form if required.
7. Complete First Article Checklist per WI32-786.
8. Package product according to requirements.
9. Combine all required submission documents in a three-ring binder per WI32-677.

10. Draft cover First Article Submission letter per WI32-822.

11. Ship First Article Products or Parts to the customer as per their requirements documented in the job folder.

Bill could only shake his head at Rapid Products's supplier requirements. It seemed that Rapid Products was asking their suppliers for something that Rapid Products couldn't do themselves! At the next break, Bill ran to his office to check his e-mail. He was surprised to discover that there was only one request for proposal (RFP) in his email basket. He passed this RFP along to Jim, and went back to the Supplier Day session, and caught up with Bill.

"Hey Sam, good news, I didn't have as many RFP's as I thought. I think I'll sit in on the rest of the Supplier Day session," said Bill.

"Not having very many RFP's doesn't sound like good news, but I'm glad you can stay," replied Sam.

"Yea, I guess you're right; with no RFP's we'll have no future orders, but I'm a glass half full guy, this may allow me to attend the joint Lean Sigma event next week! Let's get back to the session," exclaimed Bill.

Bill sat through the rest of the Supplier Day session, and thanked Sam for inviting him. The two leaders agreed to work out the details for Bill to participate in the joint Lean Sigma event planned for the next week.

Bill was starting to understand why Sam invited him to the Supplier Day session. He knew he had to do something different with his sales teams and this might just be the time to do it.

Discussion Questions

1. Discuss the similarities and differences between Lean, Six Sigma, and Lean Sigma. Which of these is most applicable to the sales process and why?

2. Why is it necessary to understand the building blocks in order to understand what Lean Sigma is? Discuss briefly the building blocks and how it can help your organization to get prepared for the Lean Sigma journey.

3. Discuss the overriding philosophies and three key Lean Sigma principles. What can Bill or your organization learn from them?

4. What do you think of this statement, "in planning your Lean Sigma transformation, be careful not to keep your expectation too low"? What are some of the outcomes you would expect your organization to achieve if they implemented Lean Sigma?

5. What are your thoughts about the "First Article Approval process?" Do you agree that the typical sales process should start with opportunity identification and end with product or first article delivery? Why or why not?

CHAPTER 3

Lean Sigma Methods and Tools: Basic Concepts

The joint supplier and Rapid Products Lean Sigma or Rapid Improvement Event (RIE) event began with introductions and expectations. During the introductions, Bill noticed that the SM from their supplier was attending the Lean Sigma RIE sessions, and made a note to catch up with him to pick his brain about Lean Sigma methods and tools for sales processes.

The planned agenda for the three-day event is shown as follows.

Day 1
1. Welcome and introductions.
2. Review logistics of the RIE.
3. Review objectives of the RIE.
4. Conduct Lean Sigma overview training.
5. Review any baseline measurements and key performance indicators.
6. Data collection and subsequent analysis as required.
7. Complete next day planning.

Day 2
1. Complete process and data analysis.
2. Develop proposed improvements.
3. Identify potential roadblocks to improvements.
4. Implement improvement trials.
5. Communicate with others who are affected.
6. Address potential roadblocks.
7. Complete next day planning.

Day 3
1. Run final trials.
2. Implement final improvements.
3. Develop standard work documents.
4. Conduct training as required.
5. Create open items list.
6. Identify plan for the future.
7. Prepare a management report and lessons learned wrap up.
8. Conclude the RIE.

RIEs are sometimes called Kaizen events. RIEs are characterized by the following.

Rapid Improvement Events

RIEs, sometimes called "Kaizen" events or "Kaizen Blitzes," are targeted events conducted by improvement teams to implement improvements quickly, in a specific area. Teams use RIEs to implement significant improvements in a relatively short time-frame. Depending on the scope of the improvement targeted, RIEs can last anywhere from one to two hours to three to five days.

RIEs are used instead of slower, incremental changes in the following circumstances.

Circumstances for RIEs
- Improvement needs are urgent or at crisis levels.
- The area being addressed is continually in use by the organization, and taking the area out of service can only be tolerated for a short duration.
- Only a short duration of training and facilitation can be afforded due to time or financial constraints.
- There is a very narrow area of focus.

As with any improvement event, RIEs take preplanning, execution, and post-event follow-up to be successful. A typical RIE planning and execution flow is as follows. Use these to assist with leading a successful RIE.

RIE Planning and Execution Flow

A. Management actions (at least two weeks before RIE)

  1. Select an area, process, or product related to the Project Charter for rapid improvement.

  2. Map the current state value stream.

  3. Assess opportunities and needs with current state measurement and analytical Lean Sigma tools.

  4. Establish short-term RIE improvement measures and goals.

  5. Select a facilitator or leader.

  6. Set the RIE date(s).

B. Facilitator actions (two weeks before the RIE)

  1. Inform the area or group leader.

  2. Coordinate the RIE with the planner and/or scheduler.

  3. Invite outside participants if required.

C. Facilitator and team actions (one week before the RIE)

  1. Create or obtain current flow chart of the process to improve.

  2. Obtain current state or base-line measurements.

  3. Communicate and obtain alignment on RIE objectives.

  4. Start a log of NVA activities in the area to address.

D. Facilitator actions (pre-RIE)

  1. Create RIE work session agendas and timelines.

  2. Arrange RIE facilities and amenities.

E. RIE Day(s)

  1. Provide Lean Sigma overview training and RIE orientation.

  2. Implement improvements using plan, do, check, act (PDCA) process.

  3. Document open item action plans and follow up plan.

  4. Report out as required.

F. Facilitator (one week after the RIE)

  1. Follow-up on open item action plans.

G. Management (one month after RIE)

  1. Audit process improvements to goals.

Source: Ptacek and Motwani.

Rapid Products's senior buyer Jim Coval facilitated the RIE, and provided Lean Sigma overview and refresher training for the group. This information was still fresh in Bill's mind from the Supplier Day session the previous week. Jim also provided a detailed explanation of the 12 wastes as noted in the following.

Twelve Forms of Waste: The Dirty Dozen

Lean Sigma tools and concepts assist employees (and customers in service processes) in identifying and eliminating all types of waste. It is critical that employees have a fundamental knowledge and understanding of waste in order to identify and eliminate it. The purpose of Lean Sigma practices is to identify, analyze, and eliminate all sources of process inefficiency.

The following table was a handout Bill received in the Supplier Day Lean Sigma training session. The table summarizes the 12 wastes with examples.

The Dirty Dozen: Twelve Forms of Waste

Form	Description	Examples	Ways to eliminate
Overproduction	More than is required is made or served	• E-mailing, faxing the same document multiple times • Ineffective meetings	• Take time • Proof of need survey • Make to order
Expertise	Underutilization due to placement of people into positions where their knowledge, skills, and abilities aren't used to the fullest	• Workloads not being completed due to lack of cross-training • Assigning employees two jobs due to understaffing	• Standard work • Lean Sigma file system • Business case for Lean Sigma • Office quick-starts
Transport	Any transport of files, information, or materials	• Delivering unneeded documents • Updating customer records in different systems	• 5S • Value stream mapping • Standard work • Lean Sigma file system • Visual controls • Co-location of workers

The Dirty Dozen: Twelve Forms of Waste (Continued)

Form	Description	Examples	Ways to eliminate
Inventory	Excessive piles of paperwork, computer files, supplies, and time spent searching for documents	• Files awaiting signatures or approvals • Keeping multiple copies of reports	• 5S • Value stream mapping • Standard work • Lean Sigma file system • Kanbans for office supplies • Level loading-heijunka
Motion	Any movement of people, paper, and/or electronic exchanges that does not add value	• Hand carrying paper to another process • Using an excessive number of transaction screens to support decision making	• Standard work • New office layout • Kanbans for office supplies • Pull systems and supermarkets
Corrections	All processing required in creating a defect and the additional work required to correct it	• Data entry errors • Not having integrated IT systems	• Standard work • Lean Sigma file system • Visual controls • Mistake proofing
Overprocessing	Putting more work or effort than required into the work requested by internal or external customers	• Duplicative reports or information • Constantly revising documents • Excessive approvals	• Standard work • Lean Sigma file system • Data collection techniques • Document tagging
Waiting	Waiting for anything (people, signatures, information, etc.)	• Excessive signatures or approvals • Delay in feedback from high-level management • Waiting for a meeting to make a decision	• Value stream mapping • 5S • Lean Sigma file system • Runners • Pitch • Standard work • Scoreboards

(continued)

The Dirty Dozen: Twelve Forms of Waste (Continued)

Form	Description	Examples	Ways to eliminate
Overload	Overburdening or overloading a work system, machine, or process	• An 18 person bus carrying 25 people • A new contract requiring 80 additional hours of work and not enough staff to complete the work	• Standard work • One piece flow • Statistical analysis • Work load balancing
Unevenness	Lack of consistent flow of inputs/ information/ scheduled work from upstream processes causing many of the other types of waste previously mentioned	• Scheduling all work to be completed at the end of the month and not during the month at even intervals • Poor office processes for locating documents when a staff member is on leave	• 5S • Value stream mapping • Standard work • Work load balancing
Environmental	Any waste that is generated by a service organization that impacts the environment, whether it is heat, solid, liquid, or gas	• Paper or plastic used in a cafeteria that isn't recycled • Unnecessary use of power when machines and equipment aren't in use	• Reduce, reuse, recycle • Sustainability or green metrics
Social	Waste from the other areas of society, such as poverty, discrimination, malpractice, health and injuries, nutrition, literacy and education, and also waste on account of social media networking	• Time spent by employees at work socializing • Advertising products on social networking sites that are not read by target audience	• PDCA • Sustainability metrics • Performance/gap analysis

Bill thought about where these wastes could be present in the sales department, and made the following notes.

1 of 12. The Waste of Overproduction

Producing some type of work prior to it being required is waste of overproduction. Providing a service above and beyond what is needed is also considered overproduction. Overproduction is when too much of something is made or served. This is the greatest of all the wastes. Overproduction of work or services can cause other wastes. For example, by preparing extra copies of a report, you are using extra paper, extra time to handle the reports, and extra motion and transportation to dispose of the reports, and so on. Activities without direct immediate purpose should be eliminated or reconfigured, unless they are already understood as essential to a perfect process.

2 of 12. The Waste of Expertise

The underutilization of people's expertise is a result of not placing people where they can (and will) use their knowledge, skills, and abilities to the fullest providing value-added work and services. An effective performance management system will reduce this waste significantly. Use company policies and procedures to effectively place people where they will most benefit the organization.

3 of 12. The Waste of Transport

Excess transport affects the time of delivery of any work within an office. Even with Internet and e-mail readily available, too often, or not often enough, documents (i.e., files) that provide little or no value are moved downstream regardless of need. Reducing or eliminating excess transport waste is important. Locating all work in sequential process operations and as physically close together as possible will help eliminate or reduce this waste. Transport between processes that cannot be eliminated should be automated as much as possible. Ask questions such as: "Is the office layout optimal?," "Is the release and request for work automated?," and "Is IT aware of the problem and can they help?"

4 of 12. The Waste of Inventory

Excessive piles of paperwork, computer files, supplies, and time spent searching for a document is waste. They all take up space or require someone's time. If a document is waiting for additional information (i.e., signature, review, approval, etc.) and there is a change, then the time the document has been waiting is waste. There are basically two types of inventory waste related to administrative areas: (1) office supplies and (2) information.

5 of 12. The Waste of Motion

Any movement of people that does not add value is waste. This waste is created by poor office layout or design, faulty or outdated office equipment, supply inaccessibility, and movement of information or data that does not add value. The waste of motion is insidious and is hidden in service procedures that have not been reviewed for continuous improvement initiatives. Regardless of the industry, motion waste may appear as someone who is looking "busy" but not adding value to the work or service. Lean Sigma tools will assist to identify, reduce, or eliminate this waste.

6 of 12. The Waste of Corrections

Correction waste refers to all processing required in creating a defect or mistake and the additional work required to correct a defect. Defects (either internal or external) result in additional administrative processing that will add *no* value to the product or service. It takes less time to do work correctly the first time than the time it would take to do it over. Rework and corrections are wastes and add more costs to any product or service for which the customer will not pay. This waste can reduce profits significantly.

7 of 12. The Waste of Overprocessing

Putting more work or effort into the work required by internal or external customers is waste. Excessive processing does not add value for the customer and the customer will not pay for it. This is one of the most difficult administrative wastes to uncover. Some questions to ask to assist in the identification of this waste are: "What are the most basic processes required to meet the customer needs?" or "Is there a clear understanding of the customer's needs?"

8 of 12. The Waste of Waiting

Waiting for anything (people, signatures, information, etc.) is waste. This waste of waiting is "low hanging fruit," which is easy to reach and ripe for the taking. We often do not think of paper sitting in an in-basket or an unread e-mail as waste. However, when looking for the item (document or e-mail), how many times do we mull through that in-basket or the Inbox and try to find it? How many times do you actually touch something before it is completed? It is the finish it, file it, or throw it away system that can help eliminate this waste. This waste is closely related to "wasting time."

9 of 12. The Waste of Overload

The overburdening or overloading of a work system or process typically causes other wastes to occur. Overload must be handled as a separate waste as it can be identified easily during the value mapping process, and is often expressed in terms of capacities of equipment or people. Usually this waste causes a great sense of frustration and aggravation for customers and employees, and often leads to other wastes and loss sales.

10 of 12. The Waste of Unevenness

Lack of a consistent flow of inputs, information, or scheduled work from upstream processes causes many of the other types of waste previously mentioned. Unevenness such as traffic jams, loading and unloading rental car busses, lunch-hour rushes, and the like create special needs for organizations wanting to provide the highest level of service.

11 of 12. Environmental Waste

As organizations become more sustainable or "Green," they have to make extra efforts to protect the environmental resources as they are becoming very scarce. Any waste that is generated by an organization that impacts the environment, whether it is, heat, solid, liquid, or gas is classified as environmental waste. These items can be observed in an organization's trash containers and dumpsters.

12 of 12. Social Waste

Social waste is another category of waste that sales organizations need to focus on if they wish to become more sustainable. The term social waste is broad and includes areas such as poverty, discrimination, malpractices, health and injuries, nutrition, literacy and education, and also waste on account of social media networking. When people who are supposed to be working are using their social media when not allowed, or when an organization is not capitalizing on the use of social media applications where appropriate. Bill felt this was a key opportunity for his sales teams.

Bill knew that each of the 12 wastes existed for his sales organization, and recalled the leading waste questions identified in Supplier Day session noted in the following:

1. Where is waste causing us to spend excess time, resources, and money?
2. How can I communicate these wastes throughout the organization?
3. What are some of the obvious wastes (low-hanging fruit)?
4. What can be done to immediately improve customer satisfaction?

Bill thought he'd use these questions to stimulate people and promote more open communications regarding waste and continuous improvements in the sales areas.

As a learning exercise, the RIE team completed a virtual waste walk on the following Lean Sigma Service Excellence "Waste Walk" form. The form can be used by teams or individuals to identify waste in their work environments. Simply take the form into the work environment, and look for a waste or two in each of the "Dirty Dozen" waste categories. This exercise develops a deeper understanding for waste, and may provide a starting point for an initial project. At a minimum, the results will stimulate discussion, learning, and waste observation. Bill thought about how he could use this form to help teach his sales team about wastes and continuous improvement opportunities.

Lean Sigma Service Excellence Waste Walk Checklist

Types of waste	Waste observations
Overproduction Producing more material or information than is needed or used	
Expertise Not using people's minds and getting them involved	
Transport Moving tools and materials to the point of use	
Inventory Materials or information. This includes all work in process and finished goods	
Motion Movement of people. This includes walking or riding, as well as smaller movements	
Corrections This includes rework or fixing of products or information that is wrong the first time	
Overprocessing This includes work above and beyond the minimum requirements or needs	
Waiting This includes any time delayed or waiting for materials, information, or people	
Overload This is when workload is too much and machines break, and people burnout	
Unevenness This is when workload varies from slow to fast uncontrollably	
Environmental This includes pollution and other wastes of the environment	
Social This is waste that impacts social issues	

Jim provided the following outline about Lean Sigma methods and tools. Bill thought that this outline would also help his sales team understand how to apply Lean Sigma in the sales area.

Lean Sigma Methods

The Lean Sigma methods used for Lean Sigma transformations include a systematic approach or steps to initiate improvement in an organization. The systematic approach is defined at three levels of engagement. Each level must use the PDCA improvement process.

Leadership Level:
- Develop Lean Sigma understanding and commitment for organization leaders.
- Develop and communicate Lean Sigma Strategy to the organization.
- Develop and deploy a tactical plan to transform the organization into a Lean Sigma enterprise.
- Set, align, and communicate measureable goals and rewards to sustain and support the Lean Sigma enterprise and thinking.
- Conduct regular organizational performance reviews.

Project, Systems, or Team Level:
Use the define-measure-analyze-improve-control (DMAIC) improvement process. The DMAIC improvement process phases are defined as follows:
- *Define* the project scope, resources, and objectives.
- *Measure* the current state process key performance measures drivers, capabilities, flows, and outcomes.
- *Analyze* the current state process data to identify and prioritize improvement opportunities.
- *Improve* the process by applying Lean Sigma improvement tools and techniques.
- *Control* the process so that the improvements are sustainable.

Worker Level:

1. Implement a housekeeping and visual control effort at all worksite(s).
2. Conduct hourly or daily mini-experiments to improve processes.

By engaging at these three levels, an organization can truly begin to transform their culture to a continuous improvement-driven environment.

Lean Sigma Tools

Bill reviewed the following Lean Sigma Tool Application Chart distributed during the session.

The following Lean Sigma Tool Application Grid is not all inclusive. It covers the Lean Sigma tools identified in the applications chart. These tools are found to be the most applicable for organizations. Not all Lean Sigma tools will work the same in every environment. Lean Sigma tools that apply directly in a mass production manufacturing environment apply to a service environment, but might not be a direct fit. Just as one would not use a screwdriver to loosen a hex-head bolt, not every Lean Sigma tool will apply to every environment and culture. The savvy Lean Sigma practitioner will identify the key applicable Lean Sigma tools, and apply them as needed.

Bill thought the Lean Sigma overview training would never end and he was glad to get on to the working portion of the RIE. The first step was to review the data gathered on the customer phone order process, which is the target process to improve for this RIE. The following data represent data collected during the previous three-week period. This data collection was part of the pre-event preparation.

The value added (VA) versus nonvalue added (NVA) analysis is used to illuminate the waste in a process. Once the process steps are documented, VA and NVA times can be measured and placed into a simple data table to compare the VA content to NVA time content. When conducting time studies, do not be overly concerned with whether the time is from the fastest or slowest person. Take as accurate measurements as can be obtained, and document them. If there is concern regarding the relative speed of an individual, simply document the concern in the Opportunity Log as a concern. The fact that there is variation may be an opportunity for making improvements to the standards.

DMAIC Alphabetical Tool Application Chart

		Lean Sigma improvement phases				
Lean Sigma tools		**Define**	**Measure**	**Analyze**	**Improve**	**Control**
1	5Ss				X	X
2	5-Whys		X	X		
4	Cause and effect diagrams	X	X	X		
5	Check sheets		X			X
6	Constraint or Bottleneck analysis		X	X		
7	Cross-training to develop worker flexibility				X	X
8	Flow, process, Swim lane, or value stream maps	X	X	X	X	
10	Frequency charts		X			X
11	Future state flow maps				X	
12	Histograms		X	X	X	X
15	Key metric data profiles		X	X		X
16	Leveling service flow, pull signals (kanbans), and paced work flow (Heijunka)				X	X
17	Mass customization				X	
18	Mistake proofing (Poka yoke)				X	X
20	Pareto and pie charts		X	X		X
21	Performance management and improvement				X	X
22	Plan–Do–Check–Act process		X	X	X	X
23	Problem solving—Corrective and preventative actions		X	X	X	X

DMAIC Alphabetical Tool Application Chart (Continued)

	Lean Sigma tools	Lean Sigma improvement phases				
		Define	Measure	Analyze	Improve	Control
26	Quality function deployment (QFD)	X	X			
27	Queue time		X	X	X	X
28	Radar chart		X	X		X
29	Rapid improvement events				X	
30	Run and control charts		X	X		X
31	Scatter plots			X		
32	Spreadsheets and pivot tables		X	X		X
33	Standard work for leaders			X	X	X
34	Standardized work			X	X	X
35	Statistical process controls		X	X		X
37	Supplier/Input > Process > Output/Customer (SIPOC)	X	X	X		
38	Talk time, predictive selling or service rate analysis		X	X	X	
39	Value-added versus non-value-added analysis		X	X	X	
40	Visual controls				X	X
41	Visual management and performance scoreboards		X	X	X	X
42	Voice of the customer (VOC)	X	X			X

Source: Ptacek and Motwani.

The following table is an example of a VA versus NVA analysis for a customer phone order process.

Customer Phone Order Process Data

Process step	Process name	Type	Begin time	Operation time	End time	Value add?	Value add total
1	Answer phone	Process	0:00	0:00:25	0:00:25	Yes	0:00:25
2	Ask for customer information	Process	0:00	0:00:40	0:01:05	Yes	0:01:05
3	Does customer have account	Process	0:01	0:00:05	0:01:10	Yes	0:01:10
4	Place on hold and forward	Transport	0:01	0:01:15	0:02:25	No	0:01:10
5	Ask for customer information	Process	0:02	0:00:20	0:02:45	No	0:01:10
6	Take information for credit app	Process	0:02	0:03:45	0:06:30	Yes	0:04:55
7	Wait for credit approval	Delay	0:06	0:06:05	0:12:35	No	0:04:55
8	Approved?	Decision	0:12	0:00:00	0:12:35	Yes	0:04:55
9	Ask for customer information	Process	0:12	0:00:40	0:13:15	No	0:04:55
10	Does customer have account	Process	0:13	0:00:05	0:13:20	No	0:04:55
11	Determine product needs	Process	0:13	0:01:30	0:14:50	Yes	0:06:25
12	Is product on hand?	Process	0:14	0:00:15	0:15:05	No	0:06:25
13	Check system for lead time	Process	0:15	0:00:10	0:15:15	No	0:06:25

(continued)

Customer Phone Order Process Data (Continued)

Process step	Process name	Type	Begin time	Operation time	End time	Value add?	Value add total
14	Quote lead time to customer	Process	0:15	0:00:05	0:15:20	No	0:06:25
15	Is lead time acceptable?	Process	0:15	0:00:00	0:15:20	No	0:06:25
16	Contact operations for LT information	Process	0:15	0:07:35	0:22:55	No	0:06:25
17	Is lead time acceptable?	Process	0:22	0:00:00	0:22:55	No	0:06:25
18	Place order	Process	0:22	0:01:45	0:24:40	Yes	0:08:10
19	Validate customer ship info	Inspect	0:24	0:00:30	0:25:10	No	0:08:10
20	Thank customer	Process	0:25	0:00:10	0:25:20	Yes	0:08:20

With the VA and NVA time table completed, various charts can be constructed to illuminate the waste, and identify opportunities for improvement. The VA to NVA comparison charts subsequently are for the previous VA versus NVA table.

Summary	
Value-added time	0:08:20
Total time	0:25:20
% Non-value added	67%
% Value added	33%

Process type breakdown	
Process time	0:17:30
Delay time	0:06:05
Transport time	0:01:15
Inspection time	0:00:30

These data can be plotted in a simple chart for more visual impact. The visual impact helps the improvement team "see" the opportunities.

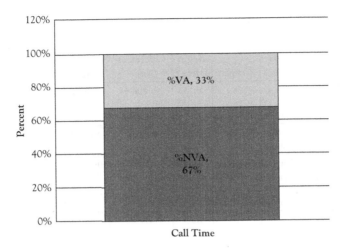

VA and NVA stacked bar chart

With this data documented, Jim conducted a brief training session on VSMs, and developed the following current state map (CSM) and flow diagram for Rapid Products's phone ordering process which was the target improvement area for this RIE.

Bill noted similarities and differences between the value stream map and the flow diagram. The value stream map groups process steps in value-added groups, while the flow diagram more closely follows the tabular data as indicated by the previous VA versus NVA Analysis table.

It is common to construct both a value stream map and a flow diagram to thoroughly analyze the processes being improved upon. However, this is not always the case. The value stream map and process flow diagram assist to visually illustrate the constraints relative to the entire process flow.

By reviewing the flow diagram or the value stream map, it can be seen that there are three basic loops in the customer phone order process flow. The three process loops are as follows:

1. The standard product loop is for a customer who has an account and the product is on hand.
2. The credit approval loop is for the customer who needs to apply for credit and the product is on hand.
3. The lead time info loop is for the customer who does not require credit approval and the product is not on hand.

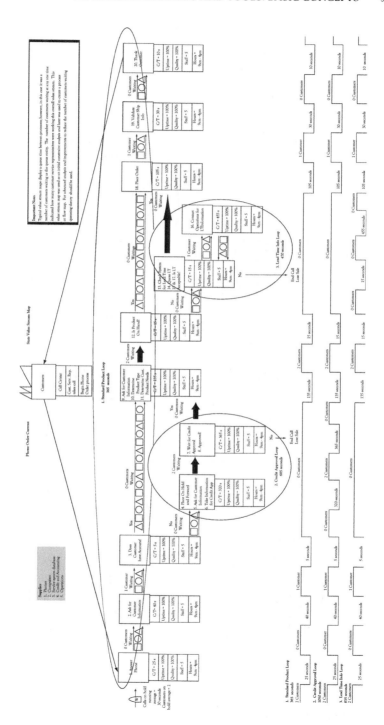

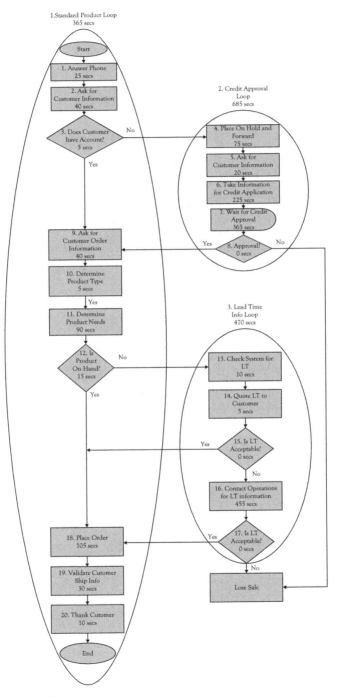

Phone Order Current

Each loop has a constraint operation. For the standard product loop (1) the constraint is "Place Order" (Step 18) at 105 seconds. For the credit approval loop (2) the constraints are "Wait for Credit Approval" (Step 7) at 365 seconds and "Take Information for Credit App" (Step 6) at 225 seconds. For the lead time info loop (3) the constraint is "Contacting Operations for LT Information" (Step 16) at 455 seconds.

By following the flow of any given order, the time for the longest operation becomes the constraint. The improvement team agreed to focus their improvement initiatives on the constraints in each process loop.

This process was refreshing for Bill, as he could begin to understand how the Lean Sigma tool of mapping and flow charting could help him define the sales process, and better understand the constraints and improvement targets for the process. He was excited to think about applying this tool to the sales process.

The phone order value stream map and flow diagram were very useful for the joint RIE team. As a result of using these tools, the improvement team came up with the following improvement opportunities:

1. Standardize the credit approval process so that up to 90 percent of credit requests can be computed by the customer service representative rather than having to call the credit department. Target time reduction is 15 percent of current state. For this improvement idea, standards for credit approval were established and posted on the organization's intranet. As customers request credit approval, customer service representatives will collect the critical credit approval information and review the data versus the credit approval standards on the intranet. It was found that many credit approval requests met the standard criteria and could be handled in this manner. If further the request fell outside the standard requirements, the customer was then transferred to the Credit Department for further analysis. This standardization improvement project still enabled the Credit Department to maintain control of the credit approval parameters, yet have most of the actual credit approval review completed by Customer Service.

2. Standardize the special lead time request process so that customer service representative can resolve up to 80 percent of the special lead

time requests of customers. Target time reduction is 10 percent of current state. For this improvement idea, standard lead time tables were established for most of the organization's product lines. Lead time standards were determined by analyzing specific Bill of Material typical lead times and processing time. The proposed standard lead times were posted on the organization's intranet system where customer service representative could access them. For items that fell outside the standard guidelines, or where a customer could not accept the improved lead-time, the customer service representative would call operations. This lead time improvement standardization project required operations to establish weekly lead time guidelines.

3. Implement pull signals on more standard items and standard materials, to ensure product availability. The target here is to have up to 80 percent of standard items in a supermarket inventory system. By holding supermarkets of key raw materials, operations could produce to order faster and reduce lead times. Simple pull signals were implemented in the raw material area. In the finished goods area, an analysis of annual usage and seasonality by model was completed. The organization developed a schedule for putting pull cards in place that would better match the seasonality of product demand. By following the standard schedule for supermarket pull cards, the organization was able to minimize their inventories.

The rest of the RIE days would be spend implementing the improvement ideas, and documenting a path forward for improvements. Near the end of the first day, Bill finally had a chance to catch up with the supplier's sales manager. Bill introduced himself to Ray, and they hit it off very well. It seems sales people are cut from the same cloth.

Discussion Questions

1. Do your organizations host Rapid Improvement Events (RIE)? Do you find them beneficial? What are your thoughts about the RIE flow presented?

2. By means of examples, please explain the Twelve Forms of Waste. Which of these wastes do you encounter most often? Why do you

think it is critical for the management of every organization to identify the different waste using the Waste Walk Checklist?

3. Why is it important that a Lean transformation be conducted at three levels?

4. Identify the similarities and differences between the value stream map and the flow diagram. What has been your experience with these diagrams? What do you think of Bill's approach toward them?

5. Evaluate the process and opportunities followed and identified by the improvement team? Do you think they have made good progress?

CHAPTER 4

Comparing Manufacturing and Sales Processes

At break, Bill approached Ray, the sales manager from the Pigments Plus Company, a key pigment supplier to Rapid Products. Bill reached out his hand to shake and said "Ray?"

"Yes, I'm Ray, and you are?" replied Ray.

"I'm Bill Kecat. I manage the sales group here at Rapid Products. I've wanted to catch up to you; Sam indicates that you've been on the Lean Sigma for sales journey for a while, and that I might be able to learn some things from you. Do you have a minute for me to pick your brain?" responded Bill.

"Sure, until the session starts again," said Ray.

"Well, first off, how long have you been doing this Lean Sigma thing?" asked Bill.

Ray smiled and said, "Great question; we've been doing Sales process improvement ever since Sam required it about three years ago. At the supplier conference three years ago, Sam made it a requirement for us to align with Rapid Products regarding your Lean Sigma improvement efforts. That meant that we had to provide proposals and quotations that included cost reductions, and the best way to do that was to embrace the Lean Sigma improvement methods. At the sessions, Sam provided additional training, much like they are doing this year," professed Ray. Ray continued, "We not only used the improvement tools to in manufacturing to develop cost reductions over the life of the contract, we decided to incorporate the methods and tools into our sales processes as well."

"Yeah, we use the methods and tools in manufacturing, and have been quite successful, but I'm not sure it applies to sales," indicated Bill.

"Oh absolutely it applies to sales! Perhaps even more so; it is a bit different than in manufacturing, but the methods and tools helped us to eliminate wastes and grow sales faster that we would have been able to do without them," exclaimed Ray.

"I see Rapid Products use the Lean Sigma methods and tools in our manufacturing areas. In our manufacturing areas, we have cycle times, scrap, inventory and we've been reducing them for a while, but how does it apply in sales areas?" asked Bill.

"Well remember the 12 wastes? These wastes exist in sales as well, they just look different than they do in manufacturing," said Ray.

"Yeah, I do see that, even in this phone order rapid improvement event I've seen several forms of waste are present and being reduced or eliminated," replied Bill.

"Well when we mapped our sales processes, we found we had almost every type of waste. We overproduced several reports on a weekly basis that no one read or used, we had people assigned to the wrong areas wasting their expertise, and we were spending way too much time driving to sales calls, when most of our customers didn't really need to see us, but in reality, they were paying indirectly for our visits. We also had a fairly high error or correction rate on our proposals, and we eventually completely modified our sales organization structure based on what we discovered with Lean Sigma methods. At next break I can share more with you. We should get back to the session now," said Ray.

At the next break Bill and Ray reconnected, and Ray explained his perspective on sales processes. "You see sales processes are not really that different than manufacturing processes. Yeah, manufacturing processes generally have a product, but don't we supply a product as well? Isn't a proposal or quotation a product? We have to conform to standards and specifications, and deadlines as well. Sales processes have inputs, and suppliers, starting points, process steps, and end points, as well as outputs and customers. The inputs for a manufacturing process may be materials and specifications, while inputs for a sales process are typically information and possibly some forms. Manufacturing processes have these items as well. You see sales processes are simply service processes. We use what we call a 'counselor selling' approach, where we try to provide client counseling on problem solving whether it involves our products or services or not. We believe that if we act in the best interest of the client we will be seen by them as problem solvers, not just suppliers. Being a counselor seller is like providing a problem solving service. When we were just starting Lean Sigma in sales we went to a Lean Sigma for Service seminar and learned about the following areas of service."

"It's not always about speed and efficiency for a service organization," continued Ray. "Sometimes service customers detailed proposals; sometimes they just want rough numbers. All requests for quotes are not the same. Ray continued, "For example, we used to treat every request for quote the same no matter what we were being asked for. Our quote process took only 24 hours to complete based on the data we were given by the customer, but we found sometimes this process was too long, so we developed a quick quote process with standards and the like."

Bill smiled a knowing smile and said, "We do that too, but we are never really sure why, and lately our quick quote process has been used more and more regardless of what was requested by the customer. It seems the sales person drives the process."

"I can see where this might cause some problems for you," replied Ray.

"How do you know what your customers want?" asked Ray.

"What do you mean?" asked Bill, seeming a bit confused by the question. "They send a request for quote."

"Well, how do you know if the customer wants a quick quote or a fully detailed quote?" clarified Ray.

"Well, we assume the sales person knows. We develop relationships and trust our gut on what is needed. Sometimes, if we have a good relationship, we may call and ask specifically what they want. Otherwise, we just get the proposal or quote turned around as fast as possible, as sometimes the first quote back gets the order," said Bill.

"That seems a bit risky to me," replied Ray. "Sales quality differs from product quality in that sales specifications and requirements are not always as clearly defined or articulated by the customer or buyer. In fact, it is quite common for customers of the same sales organization, to have completely different expectations and requirements. You claim that the relationship dictates the process, but that can cause variation based on the relationships, and Lean Sigma methods work to reduce variation and errors. Sales organizations must, therefore, discover and define their own service quality parameters, measures, and specifications based on specific customer needs, and then design systems to accommodate all potential customers, in effort to achieve a high level of customer satisfaction. Sales organizations need to consider rapid identification and customization or adaptation to the client's desires," Ray continued.

"Quality in general is often confused with product or service features. For example, a person may consider a Hilton hotel to be a higher quality than a Motel 6. These two lodging providers each provide similar base services, yet the Hilton may offer additional features along with overnight accommodations. They each have specifications and requirements designed for different target markets or customers. They each can provide quality facilities and services to meet their client's needs," added Ray.

Ray continued, "Features such as swimming pools, fitness rooms, dining rooms, office services, etcetera, are considered additional features, not improved quality. A guest wanting only an inexpensive, clean, and safe place to sleep for the night may be perfectly satisfied, and even delighted, with a high quality room at a Motel 6. Each provider may have equally high quality in the services and features they provide."

"Sales deliverables themselves can be complex and subjective with many stakeholders. Sales deliverables can be characterized by the following general parameters," said Ray as he picked up a marker and wrote the following on the white board.

Sales Deliverables

Sales and Service Deliverables Parameters

- Integrity and trust worthiness: Making and honoring commitments, deadlines and expectations.
- Timeliness: Delivery of service or information in a reasonable time frame.
- Courtesy: Being respectful and courteous in service or information delivery.
- Consistency: Having similar and consistent results met each service or sales transaction.

- Predictability: Meeting normal expectations in a predictable fashion.
- Accessibility: Being accessible to the client when they need to meet or communicate.
- Completeness: Resolving issues and providing services as agreed upon.
- Clarity: Providing clear and unambiguous service, instruction or information. Defining expectations and outcomes clearly.
- Value: Providing a fair and reasonable service deliverable for the fees incurred.
- Hassle, annoyance or waste-free transmission: Providing sales processes and services that do not frustrate the consumer or client.
- Accuracy: Providing accurate information and results or outcomes.
- Cleanliness: Providing clean facilities or equipment for client use and interaction.
- Enjoyment or satisfaction realized: How a service or transaction makes a person feel.

"In identifying and defining client specifications, and requirements, sales organizations should consider these parameters, and make sure that they are appropriately satisfied," concluded Ray.

"Yea, I get all that, and that's why we focus on relationships," added Bill. He continued, "Some sales process deliverables or outcomes are more objective or measureable than others. For example, a sales representative can deliver a quotation quickly, but if it is inaccurate or has to be modified several times, this can frustrate a potential customer, and I think this may be the source of some of our problems."

Bill grabbed the pen from Ray and sketched the following diagram on the whiteboard. Bill explained the diagram by saying, "This diagram plots the ability to objectively measure the service outcome, against the type or focus of the service provided."

Bill continued, "Many sales service transactions shift fluidly during the delivery process. An example might be a communication between a customer and a bank teller while processing a deposit. The deposit being

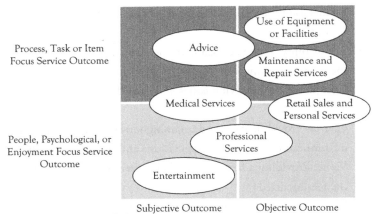

Service Outcomes and Focus
Source: Ptacek and Motwani.

entered accurately is clearly measurable, yet the 'feeling' that the customer has during the process may not be as easily measured. In fact, one customer may desire a friendly and talkative experience, and to learn about the new savings program, while the next customer does not value any chit-chat. The teller may behave the same for each of these customers, and will get good reviews from one, and poor reviews from the other. Here lies one of the keys to developing sales service excellence—understanding the customer's need, and we use our relationship building to do this."

"There are a lot of opportunities for Lean Sigma methods and tools in a sales organization. I think you should start a couple of improvement projects," commented Ray.

"Great! How do I do that? Where do I start? Where did you start?" asked Bill.

"First, you need to build a foundation to support Lean Sigma improvements in sales, so you have plenty of time. The first step starts with you," Ray said.

"Me? Why me?" replied Bill.

"The session is about to start, we'd better get back to our seats," Ray said. During the next session, Bill did not hear a word of the presentation. He was too busy running Ray's comments through his head. How could it all start with me, when I have no idea where to start? Bill wondered. He would not get that chance to ask Ray any follow up questions either, as the sessions were coming to a close, and Ray had to run immediately after the session. Bill wondered where to start. He thought he'd better catch up with Sam the following week.

Discussion Questions

1. Evaluate Bill and Ray's conversation. Do you think Ray was able to convince Bill about the application of Lean in the sales process?
2. Do you agree with Ray's comments that, "You see that sales processes are not really that different from manufacturing processes?" Why or why not? Explain.
3. Evaluate the sales and service delivery parameters identified by Ray? Which of these does you or your organization use?
4. Critically evaluate the services outcome and focus diagram. Where would your organization fit on this diagram?

CHAPTER 5

Key Enablers—Policy Deployment, Accountability Sessions, Employee Training and Involvement, and Lean Sigma Tool Selection and Application

Bill couldn't wait to get with Sam the next week, and when they connected, Bill started firing off questions.

"Sam, Ray from Pigments Plus told me Lean Sigma starts with me; but where do I start? How can I get my team trained? What process should I map first? Can you help me?" asked Bill.

"Slow down Bill. There are some additional things you should review before you get too far down the road," cautioned Sam. "I'm spending more time with you now than I do with my people. You'll have to put me on your payroll pretty soon!" said Sam jokingly. Sam reached into a file, and handed Bill a one page document. On the document was the following list.

Key Enablers for Lean Sigma Success

1. Leadership establishing, communicating, and living up to the vision, mission, and values—direction setting or setting the course and "walking the talk."
2. Resource commitment.
3. Training and education on technical, process, and people skills.
4. Process and results focused.

5. Robust policy deployment, goal alignment, and accountability systems.
6. Total system or value stream focus.
7. Employee involvement.
8. Perseverance and commitment.

Source: Lean Thinking and PPS.

Sam explained where the document came from, and each key to Bill. "Recently we visited several highly successful Lean Sigma suppliers to learn what had made each of them so successful. What we found was amazing; each company we visited generally concluded the same eight keys to success. We found that this was an enhancement to the current literature on Lean Sigma transformations," explained Sam. Sam continued and explained in greater detail each key enabler.

1. "Leadership establishing, communicating, and living up to the vision, mission, and values—Setting the course and 'walking the talk.' Lean Sigma transformations do not happen by accident. It takes leadership to identify and communicate the need to change, define what to change to, and to define a process to use to continually improve. Too often leaders will have good intentions in mind for their organizations, but do not provide the key elements for continuous improvement. The vision, mission, and values are too often either absent entirely, or placed in plaques on the lobby wall, and never really used to drive improvement and excellence. One of leadership's chief responsibilities is to create an environment where the need for continual improvement and excellence can be understood by all, and people can motivate themselves to excellence. Leaders need to communicate the current business realities and priorities to the workforce, and challenge them with delivering continuous improvement. This can be done very effectively through the vision, mission and value documents, and proper strategic planning. This starts with you Bill. This is what ray probably meant."

2. Resource commitment
   Transforming an organization to Lean Sigma takes energy. Resources such as time for team work sessions, training materials and instructors, and materials for improvement projects and

plan, do check, act (PDCA) experiments all will be required during a Lean Sigma transformation. If the proper resources are not provided, progress will slow or stop. People will perceive a lack of commitment from leadership, and people will go back to less effective ways of doing business. The continued commitment of key resources at key times is one way leaders show their resolve to transform the organization. Remember Larry, a leader's actions speak louder than their words. It helps if leaders actually participate in early events, and hold themselves accountable to use the tools for their own work too.

3. Training and education on technical, process, and people skills

"This is an enabler for Lean Sigma transformations. If people don't have the proper instruction and a systematic approach to improvement, random and sometimes detrimental results may occur. Some level of expertise needs to be developed by the leaders and key workers within an organization to fully transform an organization to a Lean Sigma environment. Not only the right materials, but the right counseling and mentors providing guidance at the right times will also support a Lean Sigma transformation. It should be expected that key leaders show their leadership by aggressively learning about Lean Sigma methods and tools. They lead the organization in Lean Sigma learning," Sam continued.

4. Process and results focused

"Process and results means not only focusing on the results or the bottom line, but also to be concerned for *how* the gains are being achieved. During the initial stages of a Lean Sigma transformation it's normal for several early successes to be realized. These are commonly referred to as 'low hanging fruit' or 'quick hit' items. While these successes should be celebrated, it's equally important for leaders to recognize and speak to the process, methods, and tools being applied. This dual focus will reinforce the workforce's commitment to follow the process to achieve results. It is also important to note that there is not always low hanging fruit. Teams diligently following the Lean Sigma improvement process methods should be celebrated regardless of the outcome. By rewarding or celebrating the process, leaders will encourage more people to follow the process, and as they do, more improvements and results will be realized eventually. Remember, process first, then results."

5. Robust policy deployment, goal alignment, and accountability systems
"Policy deployment is the process of establishing, aligning and communicating the measures, goals, and objectives throughout the organization. This provides a total 'connectedness' or alignment of the entire organization. It is the report card, or 'score,' for how things are going. If properly done, policy deployment encourages and excites people into high levels of personal and team performance. Have you seen our scoreboards in the purchasing area?" asked Sam. "Those are part of the policy deployment process," added Sam.
Sam continued.

6. Total system or value stream focus
"Total system focus forces organizations to consider flow of products, services, and people in the delivery process. Too often businesses are organized into islands or silos through the organizational chart, and communicating across islands or silos is difficult if not impossible for the well meaning worker. If nothing is done to break down departmental barriers, people will become discouraged and only do enough to get by. They will conclude that leadership really doesn't care, and ask, 'If leadership doesn't care, why should I?' The concept of total systems focus recognizes that work and value flows horizontally through organizations to service their clients."

7. Employee involvement
Employee involvement and participation is how any Lean Sigma transformation actually gets done. Management cannot simply "install" a Lean Sigma culture. People of an organization are key stakeholders in transforming the organization. When they understand why the change is needed, what to change to, and what processes to use to change, they can fully deploy their energy and efforts. It is through their efforts and actions that a Lean Sigma transformation occurs. In general, people want to be on a winning team, and when an environment exists where people can strive for improvement, where the question of "What's in it for me?" is clear and inspirational, employees will motivate themselves, and strive for excellence.
and finally,

8. Perseverance and commitment

"Lean Sigma transformations do not happen overnight. Nor are they easy. Organizational leaders must display long-term persever-ance and commitment for a full transformation to occur. Patience is needed to allow teams to progress through the define-measure-analyze-improve-control (DMAIC) process and learn though PDCA improvement cycles. Remember, not everything a continuous improvement team tries will yield positive results. Consider celebrat-ing the failures as learning opportunities. Leaders will also need to navigate issues and concern along the way. It's not enough to pur-sue Lean Sigma methods when times are good. Rather, it must be a deep rooted philosophy of applying the tools and techniques in good times and bad. Lean Sigma techniques are a way of working and behaving all the time. Once leaders shift their behaviors to Lean Sigma philosophy, the organization will begin to shift as well. Lead-ing by example is my best advice," added Sam, as he went right on to the next steps for Bill.

"Your next step Bill should be to develop a strategy to improve the sales organization, and then share this with your sales team. From there, the team can develop high level goals to help achieve the strategy, and then begin the process of cascading these goals to all areas of the organization. This process is called 'Policy Deployment,' and is a 'Key Enabler,' and might for you." Sam explained.

Bill was hoping it was easier than this, but by now, he knew he should follow Sam's advice, so Bill left and began to organize his thoughts and even-tually developed the improvement strategy for his sales area, and began the policy deployment process with the sales team as Sam described it. The basic strategy is to participatively establish key measures and goals for key sales pro-cesses, such as quoting, developing proposals, and entering an order, and then measure and post, in a dashboard fashion, the actual performance to goals for each process and sales person. Once this is done, the teams will need a method to regularly review and respond to achieve continuous improvement.

Things went well at first, but then Bill was met with some resistance in the ranks of some of his most senior sales people. One of Bill's best sales people, Mary, was first to protest.

"Bill, I used to spend my time on the road, meeting with customers. I knew their needs better, and I seemed more connected with them," she implored to Bill.

"Well, what exactly is the problem Mary?" asked Bill.

"Well, I'm so busy doing process improvement work that I'm not getting out to see my customers," explained Mary.

"Have the customers indicated that this is a problem?" asked Bill.

"No, I just feel disconnected," answered Mary.

"Well Mary, when I look at your sales dashboard, it looks like everything is going better than ever. I know this is a bit different for us all, but I need to ask you to hang in there a bit and work the improvement process," requested Bill.

"I just don't think we need this Lean Sigma thing in sales, I want to get back on the road," explained Mary.

Sam had explained to Bill that resistance to change is a natural human reaction to change, and should be expected. That people often are afraid of the "unknowns" that change can bring. People may not express their fear, but it will manifest itself in resistance. Deep down, even subconsciously, they may fear not being the expert, not being able to learn the new skill or method, having to learn something new, or the sense of loss of security due to not knowing the system. Resistance was actually a sign that real progress is being made!

Bill reviewed the managing change graph (shown below) he received at a Lean Sigma transformation training session regarding managing change, and thought to himself, "I must be doing something right, hitting a nerve somewhere, if people are starting to resist."

The lack of resistance may mean that leaders are not pushing fast or hard enough. Bill decided to stay the course, but to be sympathetic to Mary's concerns. His strategy to deal with the resistance was to focus on the people who are showing interest, and nurture and cultivate their interest, rather than those who are resisting. He was hopeful that this approach would convince people to try to engage in the improvement effort. From other training materials Bill had, he knew other strategies to deal with resistance are as follows.

- Recognize that the root of resistance is based in a fear of something and is a natural human response.

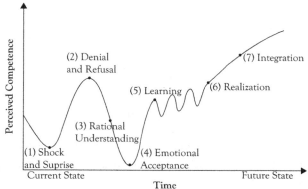

Managing Change Time Plot
Source: Ptacek and Motwani (2011).

- Answer the leading change questions; why do we need to change, what do we to change to, and how do we to do it together, and communicate this message often and consistently.
- Be honest and truthful. Do not guarantee anything except more need for change and improvement.
- Look for subtle change resistance behaviors, and address them quickly.
- Help people understand why change is needed, and to settle their fears.

With the managing change plan set, Bill led a series of sessions with his sales team. They established their mission, vision, and goals. They reviewed the company value statement, and recommitted to holding each other accountable to these standards. The sales team discussed a plan for daily work team sessions or "huddles" to discuss the day's activities and key issues. The mandate was clear; we must improve or continue to lose sales and be frustrated. Staying the current course would not lead to success. Change for the better was needed and expected from everyone. Full speed ahead with Lean Sigma was needed!

Bill felt good that his work with the sales team had addressed the key enablers. He was disappointed that it had taken nine weeks to get this done, but Sam told him to "Plan the work, and work the plan." The next step was for Bill to identify and map out the key sales processes. The maps will represent the current state, which was filled with waste and opportunities for improvement. Bill thought he'd ask Sam to attend these sessions as he thought there could be some confusion and resistance!

Discussion Questions

1. Briefly discuss the key enablers for Lean Sigma success. Why is it critical for organizations to understand these enables prior to implementation?
2. What role do you expect your leadership team to play in order to succeed in your lean transformation journey? What should Bill's or your role be?
3. What do you think of Sam's advice to Bill concerning the next step? Do you think Bill did a good job in following Sam's advice?
4. Is it normal for Bill to encounter resistance from his employees? Discuss some strategies your organization utilizes to better handle resistance to change?

CHAPTER 6

Analysis of the Current State

The day before the planned sales process mapping session, Sam caught up with Bill in the company lunch room. "So Bill, are you ready for tomorrow's sales process value stream mapping work session?" asked Sam.

"As ready as I'm going to be," replied Bill.

"They say Toyota used to be able to sketch out their value stream maps on a napkin while at lunch. So what's your basic sales process? Have you thought about that yet?" asked Sam.

"That's the problem Sam, every customer is different, every buyer is different, and as a result, every sale is a bit different. I'm not sure we'll be able to define our sales work as a process. Our process is so unique, it's like magic how we close deals!" Bill said with a grin.

"It's not magic. Every organization I've worked with claims to be unique or 'special' in some way, yet when we really look into it the core processes are very definable. I've helped a lot of sales teams with simplifying their sales process; what's your basic sales process or steps?" Sam asked.

"Well first we have to find potential customers. To do this we do advertising, marketing, we have a website, we do cold calls; there are so many things we do to identify potential new clients," stated Bill.

"For the sake of simplicity, let's call all of that 'Identifying potential new customers or clients,' " said Sam, as he grabbed a napkin and drew a box and labeled it accordingly. "What do you do next?" continued Sam.

"Well, after we identify a potential customer, we have to make contact with them," said Bill.

"We'll call that 'Engaging potential new customer,' " said Sam, as he sketched another box and labeled it accordingly. "Then what?" continued Sam.

"Then we get to know the buyer, that's where the magic starts. We have to know exactly what buttons to push, when to push, and when to stay away, this is what I call 'Sales Savvy,' " indicated Bill.

"Give me a break Bill, this is simply developing a trusting relationship. Let's call it that. What's next?" said Sam.

"I'm serious, that's a huge step, and not everyone does it the same. How can you standardize that?" asked Bill.

"Do some sales people do it better than others?" asked Sam.

"Yes, some of us have the 'magic,' and some don't," replied Bill.

"Stop calling it magic. If some people do it better than others, we can study their technique and develop basic standard work. In fact, I know this has been done already by many leading sales authors. Our customer relationship management (CRM) software is set up to help us do this better. I'm certain we can improve our process for relationship building, and train our sales people in a standardized approach to improve their techniques, and get better, more consistent results. Now let's keep moving; what comes after developing a trusting relationship?" asked Sam.

"Well, once we've made contact and used our 'magic' to start building our relationship, we work to understand what the client's needs are for our products," replied Bill with a smirk.

"Okay, let's call that 'Discovering or Creating need,' " replied Sam, as he jotted more notes on his napkin. "Then what?" added Sam.

"That's where some magic happens again; we then show and tell them how great our products and services are, and we work the magic to close a deal. In this phase we may do multiple quotes or proposals, negotiate, all in effort to close the deal. Closing the deal takes a special skill," shared Bill.

"Again, I'll bet some people do it better than others, and we can learn from them, but all that aside, the process step is really discovering the needs of the potential customer, and showing them how our products can help fill their need, solve a problem, or provide an improvement, rights? Let's call this entire mess 'Discovering Need and Advocating Solutions,' " said Sam, as he made and labeled another box on his napkin. "Is there anything else you do after closing the sale?" asked Sam.

"Yea, there's tons of stuff we do after we close the deal. We complete the new sales order forms, we stay in the loop and keep the customer informed of how we are doing, and we communicate regularly with the client; we do tons of stuff. That's why we need the big expense accounts," said Bill with a grin.

"I'll call it 'Support.' " Sam said curtly, as he added a box and label to his napkin. As Sam finished he spun the napkin around so Bill could see it and said, "There you go, this value stream map sketch is a shell of the macro sales process. I call it a shell because it has no data or details. Usually, value stream maps differ from flow charts or diagrams because of the data and details they contain. The data and details are where teams 'see the wastes.' "

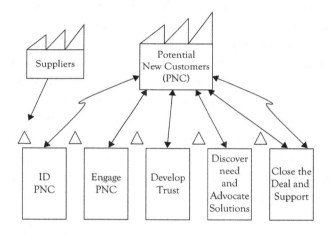

The basic outline of the macro sales process is as follows:

1. Identify potential new clients or customers
   a. Tradeshows
   b. Advertising
   c. Website
2. Engage potential new customers
   a. Arrange meeting with potential new customers
3. Developing a trusting relationship
   a. CRM
   b. Swimming with the sharks McKay
4. Discovering need and advocating solutions
   a. Dialog
   b. Questions
   c. Helping customer solve problems

  d. Counselor selling

  e. Conflict management

 5. Supporting direction or decisions

  a. Customer service

  b. Order entry and processing

Sam continued, "Now, there are several subprocesses within each of these macro sales process boxes. You and your team can use this sketch to discover where the most waste is or the poorest flow, or the greatest need for improvement, the map data and details should point you in the right direction. Once the major opportunities are identified, the team can 'drill down' and develop sub process maps as needed to discover wastes in the sub processes. This is where the team will learn what Lean tools may apply to the help improve the process. For starters, I think there is quite a bit of standard work development in the macro sale process. Maybe you could start there, and have your team address improvements at the subprocess level. When you get to your session tomorrow, let's start with this map and use it to facilitate discussion, and action planning. Now I'd say you're ready for the value stream mapping work session tomorrow. You can thank me later. I have to run. See you tomorrow." Sam said as he passed the marked up napkin to Bill, stood up, pushed his chair in and left the lunch room.

  Bill sat there a bit staring at the napkin. He thought to himself, "Wow, this really makes sense." Bill finished his lunch, grabbed the napkin, and left for his office.

  At his office, Bill began his preparation for the value stream mapping work session. He studied some of his Lean Sigma material and discovered where some basic Lean Sigma tools would apply to each of the macro sales processes. The greatest need was for standardized work in the macro value stream. Bill made note of this and finished his preparation for the work session.

  In addition to Sam, a cross-section of people from Bill's on-site sales team were invited to attend the sales value stream mapping work session. The on-site team consisted of direct sales, inside sales, and customer service. Those attending the meeting are as follows:

- Bill, the sales manager and session leader.
- Tammy, Jason, and Mary representing direct sales.

- Pat and Deb representing inside sales.
- Jack and Amy representing customer service leaders.
- Julie, Sandy, and Tom representing customer service reps.
- Sam, the supply chain manager.

Bill started the two-hour work session right on time, and shared the following agenda with the team.
Sales Process Improvement Work Session 1 Agenda

1. Overview
2. Macro sales process value map
3. Opportunity identification and prioritization
4. Action planning and next steps
5. Close

Bill welcomed everyone to the meeting, and explained why Sam was also attending. He indicated that Sam would serve as their "internal consultant." Bill got the group right to work, and made a large sketch of the shell of the macro sales value stream on the white board in a way that took up most of the board. Bill explained to the team that he wanted to use the Lean Sigma approach to improving their sales processes, and the first step was to further develop the macro sales process value stream map. To do this, the team had to populate the map shell with the data and details needed to "see the waste." Once the team clearly sees the wastes, and opportunities, they can begin to implement improvements.

Since all value stream maps begin and end with the customer, Bill began the group discussion by asking about the customer demands in term of new customers and orders processed per day, week, month, and year. As the group discussed the volume of new orders, and customers they discovered that there is quite a bit of variation in the volume of sales process transactions per day. Sam indicated that this is not all that unusual for a sales process, and encouraged the team to document the variation in the value map issues and opportunity log, and move on. Bill made the appropriate notes on the customer icon, and issues and opportunity log, and moved on to the identify potential new clients or customers process box.

Bill asked the team to think about typical value stream map process box metrics, such as Cycle Time (C/T), Change Over Time (C/O), Up Time (U/T), Quality Yield (Q), and the like, but to consider what these mean in the sales world. Also, while considering each process box, Bill wanted to capture all the subprocesses they used to complete the work for the macro process box, as well as issues, problems, and opportunities that they already know about because they actually do the work. With that Bill prompted discussion; "Tammy, you're the best I know at finding new customers, what exactly do you do to find a new customer?" asked Bill.

"Well, it's pretty straight-forward, since much of our products go directly to large retail stores, and distributors, and most of those are very well known, those accounts are basically maintenance or support accounts. To find new customers I focus on niche or boutique markets; you know, the small guys out there selling our blenders. To find them I sometimes will look search the web for specialty shops in a specific market," remarked Tammy.

Pat chimed in, "Yeah, that works, but the accounts are so small they hardly leave a dent in the overall sales numbers. I swing for the fences, and only look for accounts over $250,000 potential."

"That may explain why Tammy always wins in new customers landed, and you usually do well in sales dollars. That's why we developed the bonus around new sales dollars, and new customers," added Bill.

"Yeah, I've been meaning to talk to you about that," added Pat with a pause, and the group laughed.

Tammy interrupted the laughter, and said, "But did you know that the small accounts make up over 20 percent of our revenue?"

"Right!" added Jack from customer service, "and they take up to 80 percent of our time!"

Bill said, "Those are all good points. Let me make note of them in the process box and issues and opportunity log," and he did so.

"Okay, let's keep it moving." Bill said as he continued to facilitate the meeting.

Bill progresses process box by process box asking for the key data and details regarding the process steps, subprocesses, and known issues and opportunities.

With about five minutes left in the work session, Bill summarized the discussion, and moved on to discuss the next steps. Sam spoke up at this point and indicated that Bill should use the company A3 format to document the teams overall progress. Bill agreed that he would take responsibility for the macro map A3. The team agreed that they may need some additional training in A3's, but Sam assured them that they are very straightforward.

What Is the A3?

The A3 Report is designed to help you "tell the story" in a logical and visual way as well as be the road map for improvement and problem solving initiatives. The A3 (Report) is the size for 11 inch × 17 inch paper that is common in just about every copier made. It can be used for displaying and structuring a problem solving or continuous improvement project from beginning to end, displaying a storyboard, or be used for a report-out or briefing. It was originally developed by Toyota to simply represent a problem or improvement initiative on a one-page simple and common format.

There are typically multiple steps (i.e., categories or sections) for an A3; however, there may be more or less of them depending on how the project is structured. Keep in the mind the overall purpose for this tool is to efficiently display all the relevant information on one page (Desktop and Tablet screen) in a logical sequence as well as be a road map for your project. Relevant data or information should be represented on the A3, however, if the information does not fit, additional sheets may be used and referenced on the A3. Many times it is used to help employees "think" Lean.

The power in the A3 Report for problem solving and continuous improvement is that it provides a consistent approach (methodology) for learning and applying the Lean Six Sigma tools. It is very simple and is typically organized as a series of boxes in a template which will assist to structure your problem solving or continuous improvement process.

Or

Source: MCS Media.

At this point the macro sales value stream map (shown below) was populated with a significant amount of data. The team also had some additional data to track down, and these needs were documented on the issues and opportunities log. However, even with the map only populated

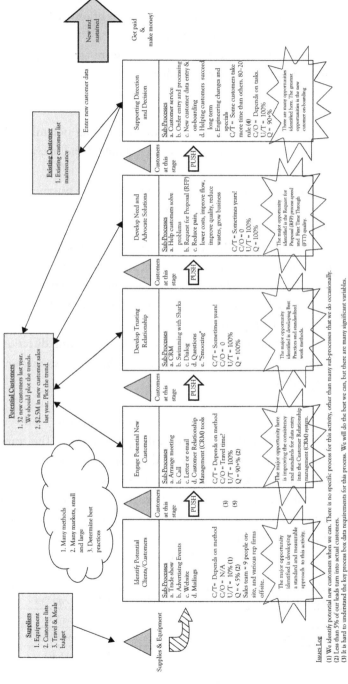

Macro Sales Pipeline CSM

with 70–80 percent of the details, the team could see the wastes and flow inhibitors coming to the surface. Together the team prioritized the next steps and made an action plan with assignments.

Bill documented the priorities by area as the team agreed on them. The completed priority list is shown as follows:

Macro Map Opportunities Priorities:

1. The major opportunity identified in the identifying potential clients and customers process is developing a standard and measurable approach to this activity.
2. The major opportunity in the engaging potential new customers area is improving the consistency and standards for data entry into the CRM system.
3. The major opportunity identified in the developing a trusting relationship are developing best practices and standardized work methods.
4. The major opportunity identified in the develop need and advocate solutions are the request for proposal (RFP) process speed and first time through (FTT) quality.
5. There are many opportunities identified in the supporting direction and decision area. The greatest opportunity is the new customer onboarding process.

Sam suggested the team break into smaller focus groups to work on improvements in each of the five major sales process areas. The team agreed, and Bill split up the work between the team members, identified area leaders, and made assignments. Each of the five teams would initiate their own A3 to document and track their progress. Bill asked each area leader to recruit their own team to address improvements. Bill also asked Sam for additional support in kicking off the five project teams, and Sam agreed. The team assignments are as follows.

Identifying potential clients and customers	Co-leaders	Tammy and Deb
Engaging potential new customers	Co-leaders	Jason and Pat
Developing a trusting relationship	Co-leaders	Mary and Sandy
Develop need and advocate solutions	Co-leaders	Jack and Julie
Supporting direction and decision	Co-leaders	Amy and Tom

Bill asked if there were any questions, and there were not. Then Bill kicked the proverbial "sleeping dog" and said that he'd like the preliminary work sessions and A3's completed in two weeks.

"Two weeks!" Jack said as he tossed his pen on the table. "I've got proposals to deliver, a customer visit next week, and then Simon in accounting wants to review the Blue water account. I can't commit to two weeks. I'm not even sure we need this in our area. This is a manufacturing tool, not a sales tool. I think we are just wasting time," Jack added.

"I hear what you're saying Jack with regard to the workload, and maybe we can get you some help there, but our company and I are committed to applying Lean Sigma tools in all areas. As I understand it, Lean Sigma methods and tools are simply ways to improve processes, and we have processes in sales, or at least we should!" replied Bill, as Jack sat visibly frustrated.

Turing to Sam, Bill asked, "Sam, any comments or words of encouragement here?"

Sam spoke up saying, "We see this quite often, where people feel the pressure of getting their regular work done and initiating a Lean Sigma effort. Once the Lean Sigma effort is in full swing, it actually becomes the way you work, and will get easier. The key is to start. Is there a timeline you could commit to Jack?"

"I don't know, at least three weeks for me to get to this," replied Jack.

"Okay, can everyone else get to this in two weeks?" asked Sam, and everyone indicated they could. Sam continued; "So two weeks for the kick-off session and A3 drafts, and three weeks for Jack's team," Jack still was not happy, and sat quietly.

Bill adjourned the session and the team filed out. After everyone left, Bill looked at Sam, and said, "What was that all about? First Mary on the metrics, now Jack on the projects, Mary's probably upset as well."

Sam grinned and said, "Stay the course Bill, they will thank you for it later. Leadership takes clear vision—stay the course friend." The two men stood, Bill shook his head, as Sam patted him on the shoulder, and they walked out of the conference room.

Discussion Questions

1. Evaluate the conversation between Sam and Bill prior to the two-hour work session. Was this conversation beneficial for Bill in identifying the basic sales process?

2. What do you think of the macro sales process developed by Sam? Do you think it is applicable to your organization? Why or why not?

3. Evaluate the sales process work session conducted by Bill. Was it productive and why? What can you learn from it?

4. Discuss the A3 report for problem solving and continuous improvement? Have you used this report? If yes, what has your experience been? If not, do you see a value in your organization using it?

5. What do you think of the process used by Bill in identifying and implementing the priority list? Explain.

CHAPTER 7

Application of Lean Sigma Tools and Results

Identifying potential clients and customers	Co-leaders	Tammy and Deb
Engaging potential new customers	Co-leaders	Jason and Pat
Developing a trusting relationship	Co-leaders	Mary and Sandy
Develop need and advocate solutions	Co-leaders	Jack and Julie
Supporting direction and decision	Co-leaders	Amy and Tom

Bill decided to attend each subteam kick-off session to make sure everyone knew that this work had his attention and is a priority, but he let the team leaders lead the sessions. Prior to the kick-off sessions, Bill worked with the team leaders to establish somewhat of a standard agenda and approach. The standard agenda below was distributed to the session participants before the meeting.

Lean Sigma Kick-Off Session Standard Agenda:

1. Welcome and purpose of the session
2. Lean Sigma overview
3. Review the macro sale current state (CS) value stream map (VSM)
4. Develop A3 for the target opportunity process
5. Develop action items, assignments, and next steps
6. Set the next session schedule
7. Adjourn

Since leading meetings or work sessions was a new requirement for many of the people, Bill also provided the teams with the following refresher training notes regarding how best to lead a meeting, and how to effectively document what was discussed during the meeting.

Meeting or work session leading is the process of presiding over, running, or facilitating a meeting to maintain focus and effectiveness. It involves establishing an agenda, identifying the necessary people to attend, scheduling a time and location, facilitating the meeting, and communicating the meeting action items and minutes.

It is wise to use a standard meeting agenda format to help you plan and stay on track during a meeting. The work session record should be initiated prior to the meeting, and include updates and status of actions items if appropriate. The teams used the following work session record as a standardized guide to follow as a work session is scheduled and conducted.

The following checklists will assist the work session leaders to prepare and lead effective meetings.

Work Session (Meeting) Prep Checklist:

1. Make sure the meeting is needed.
2. Specify and limit who should attend.
3. Distribute an agenda before the meeting, unless it's not appropriate.
4. Tell participants what preparation is expected.
5. Set an appropriate time.
6. Get started on time and keep to the schedule.
7. Try not to allow interruptions.
8. Avoid hidden agendas.

Work Session (Meeting) Leading and Facilitation Checklist:

1. Be prepared with information, copies, and so forth.
2. Welcome participants and call the session to order.
3. Restate the objective of the work session.
4. Ask for questions.
5. Explain how the session outcomes will be recorded and tracked.
6. Keep to the schedule. Ask permission to go over your scheduled ending time.
7. Invite those who haven't spoken to contribute.
8. Gain closure on each issue as you sense a consensus.
9. Document decisions, deadlines, action items, and responsibilities.

Work Session Record

Instructions: Use this page and the back to record work session occurrence. Make copies of this form and have the scribe take notes on each topic discussed. Copy the completed page(s) and distribute the completed form at the end of the work session.

Session Number: _____   Date: _____   Location: _____

Project Name: _____   Session Time: _____

Attendance	Agenda
	1. _____
	2. _____
	3. _____
	4. _____
	5. _____
	6. _____
	7. _____

Action and Agreement Register*

*Provide a brief summary of topics, discussions, agreements, or conclusions on back side if more space is needed.

Description	Who	When
1.		
2.		
3.		
4.		
5.		
6.		

Future File / Parking Lot
1.
2.
3.
4.
5.

Meeting Review
+   -

Next Work Session:
Date: Time: Location:

Recorder/Scribe:

Source: Fleming and Ptacek.

10. Summarize the outcomes.

11. Communicate next steps.

12. Distribute the minutes within one business day after the meeting.

Key Points for Work Session (Meeting) Leading:
- Make sure a work session is needed to accomplish the task or objective.
- Establish clear and objective outcomes for the work session.

- Set the agenda, start and stop times, and attendee list.
- Start and stop the work session on time. Facilitate the agenda to stay on track and allow everyone to participate. If the session is going to run long, ask for permission from the attendees to continue after the proposed end time.
- When the objectives have been met, or the session time is up, summarize the agreements, action items, the next steps, and then adjourn the session on time. If appropriate, document and distribute work session minutes.

Since the primary outcome of the kick-off sessions was the development of the A3, each team was encouraged to work section by section to populate their A3 form. To assist the teams with this, Bill thought it best to share the Macro Sales Process Improvement A3 with the teams. Bill's version took the form of the following outline.

Macro Sales Process Improvement A3 Outline

Problem or Opportunity Statement

The opportunity to address is to apply Lean Six Sigma methods and tools to our sales processes to eliminate waste and improve flow of obtaining new, and retaining existing customers, as well as improving our overall sales growth rate and profit.

Objective and Scope

The scope of this work is the entire sales process from client identification to customer service and maintenance. The objective is to apply Lean Six Sigma methods and tools to our sales processes to eliminate waste and improve flow of obtaining new, and retaining existing customers, as well as improving our overall sales growth rate and profit. The bottom line is we want to grow faster, and be more profitable, with the same (or smaller) sales resources.

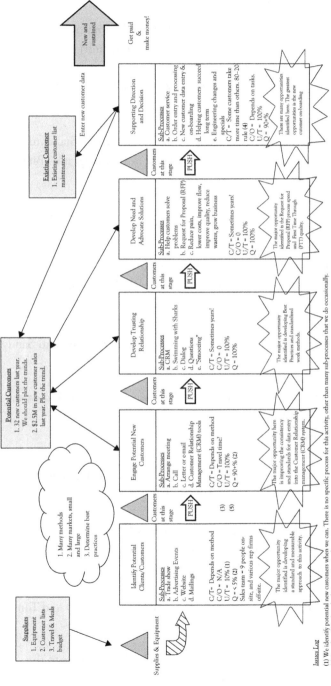

Suppliers
1. Equipment
2. Customer lists
3. Travel & Meals budget

Supplies & Equipment

1. Many methods
2. Many markets, small and large
3. Determine best practices

Identify Potential Clients/Customers

Sub-Process
a. Trade show
b. Advertising Events
c. Website
d. Mailings

C/T~ Depends on method
C/O = N/A
U/T = 10% (1)
Q = < 5% (2)
Sales team = 9 people on-site, and various rep firms offsite.

The major opportunity identified is developing a standard and measurable approach to this activity.

Customers at this stage

PUSH

(3)
(5)

Engage Potential New Customers

Sub-Processes
a. Arrange meeting
b. Call
c. Letter or e-mail
d. Customer Relationship Management (CRM) tools

C/T = Depends on method
C/O = Travel time?
U/T = 100%
Q = 90+% (2)

The major opportunity here is improving the consistency and standards for data entry into the Customer Relationship management (CRM) system.

Customers at this stage

PUSH

Potential Customers
1. 32 new customers last year. We should plot the trends.
2. $2.5M in new customer sales last year. Plot the trend.

Develop Trusting Relationship

Sub-Processes
a. CRM
b. Swimming with Sharks
c. Dialog
d. Questions
e. "Smooting"

C/T = Sometimes years!
C/O = 0
U/T = 100%
Q = 100%

The major opportunity identified is developing Best Practices and standardized work methods.

Customers at this stage

PUSH

Develop Need and Advocate Solutions

Sub-Processes
a. Help customers solve problems
b. Request for Proposal (RFP)
c. Reduce pain, lower costs, improve flow, improve quality, reduce wastes, grow business

C/T = Sometimes years!
C/O = 0
U/T = 100%
Q = 100%

The major opportunity identified is the Request for Proposal (RFP) process speed and First Time Through (FTT) quality.

Customers at this stage

PUSH

Existing Customer
1. Existing customer list maintenance

Enter new customer data

Supporting Direction and Decision

Sub-Processes
a. Customer service
b. Order entry and processing
c. New customer data entry & on-boarding
d. Helping customers succeed long term
e. Engineering changes and specials
C/T = Some customers take more time than others. 80-20 rule (4)
C/O = Depends on tasks.
U/T = 100%
Q = 90+%

There are many opportunities identified here. The greatest opportunities is the new customer on-boarding.

New and sustained

Get paid & make money!

Issues Log

(1) We identify potential new customers when we can. There is no specific process for this activity, other than many sub-processes that we do occasionally.
(2) Less than 5% of our leads turn into actual customers.
(3) It is hard to understand the key process box data requirements for this process. We will do the best we can, but there are many significant variables. We will try to tolerate the ambiguity to see where it leads.
(4) Some customers are more demanding, and take more work for the same or less sales dollars and profits.
(5) We have detailed data for many of the sub-process activities, such as the number of mailing sent, website hits, trade show costs and new client yield, person by person performance, RFP success rates, engineering changes, specials, and the like.

Current State

Ideas and Opportunities

The macro sales improvement team has broken the improvements initiatives into the following five improvement teams and target improvements.

Identifying potential clients and customers   Co-leaders   Tammy and Deb

> The target opportunity:
> - Standard and measurable approach to this activity. Standard work methods around BP's. Analytics? Scatter diagrams? Billy Ball!

Engaging potential new customers   Co-leaders   Jason and Pat

> The target opportunity:
> - Improving the consistency and standards for data entry into the customer relationship management (CRM) system.
> - Standard work for CRM data entry and accountability.

Developing a trusting relationship   Co-leaders   Mary and Sandy

> The target opportunities:
> - Best practices (BPs) and standardized work methods. Standard work around BPs.
> - Counselor selling.

Develop need and advocate solutions   Co-leaders   Jack and Julie

> The target opportunities:
> - Request for proposal (RFP) process speed. RFP standard work and processing improvements.
> - First time through (FTT) quality.

Supporting direction and decision   Co-leaders   Amy and Tom

The target opportunity:
- New customer on-boarding process. Overlaps or links to the RFP process. New standards that all tie together in the finale!

Future State

Greater sales growth rate and profitability with the same or fewer sales resources.

Future Ideas and Opportunities

None identified.

Action Plan and Timeline

The action plan includes five subteams addressing improvements in specific sales process pipeline areas. The target is for each of the five subteams to develop three- to six-month improvement implementations, with ongoing process improvements and maintenance.

Key Measures of Success

1. New sales $ per sales resource $
2. New customers per sales resource $
3. New sales $ with existing customers per sales resource $

During the kick-off sessions each of the five teams followed the standard agenda and worked to develop draft A3 outlines.

During the Identifying Potential Clients and Customers kick-off session, there was a spirited discussion with Bill. The team wanted to know exactly what Bill expected, and how they would be measured. Bill addressed these questions with the Macro Sales Process A3 content, and the team seemed satisfied. Tammy and Deb's group developed the following draft A3 outline for the identifying potential new client processes.

Identifying Potential Clients and Customers Improvement A3 Outline

Problem or Opportunity Statement

The opportunity to address is to apply Lean Six Sigma methods and tools to our identifying potential clients and customers processes to eliminate waste and improve flow. To simplify, make uniform, and get better results.

Objective and Scope

The scope of this work is our identifying potential clients and customers processes. The objective is to apply Lean Six Sigma methods and tools to this area to eliminate waste and improve flow of identifying new customers, as well as supporting the overall sales growth rate and profit improvement objectives. The bottom line is we want to be able to identify potential new customers faster and at a lower cost.

Current State

The team decided to address the improvement from an analytical approach and determine what the "ideal" customer looks like in terms of key parameters such as size, location, ordering method, distribution, special requirements, and profit. To develop this CS a great deal of data needed to be identified, collected, and analyzed. The action items from the kick-off session focused on acquiring the data.

Ideas and Opportunities

The following notes were taken in the ideas and opportunities section of the draft A3:

- Standard and measurable approach to this activity.
- Standard work methods around sales BPs.
- An analytical approach is needed. The team recalled the film "Moneyball*" 2011 film, starring Brad Pitt, where the baseball team's ownership did everything based on statistics, and improved their teams performance. The

---

*Wikipedia: **Moneyball: The Art of Winning an Unfair Game** is a book by Michael Lewis, published in 2003, about the Oakland Athletics baseball team and its general manager Billy Beane. Its focus is the team's analytical, evidence-based, sabermetric approach to assembling a competitive baseball team, despite Oakland's disadvantaged revenue situation. A film based on the book starring Brad Pitt was released in 2011.)

team believed that they too could benefit from an analytical approach.

Future State

At the kick-off session the concept of the future state was not very clear, but the team felt strongly that it centered on a targeted analytical approach to getting new customers.

Future Ideas and Opportunities

None identified.

Action Plan and Timeline

Each member took responsibility for gathering specific data needs, and the team agreed to meet on a weekly basis until something different was needed.

Key Measures of Success

The team wanted to align with the Macro A3 metrics, so they developed the supporting team metrics and measures as follows:

1. New sales $ per sales resource $
   a. Profit percent of a new account or customer
2. New customers per sales resource $
   a. Same
3. New sales $ with existing customers per sales resource $
   a. Profitability by account or customer average

Initiative Actions and Outcomes

The team collected and analyzed data regarding the idea customer. To do this they gathered information about each customer's account such as size, location, ordering method, distribution, special requirements, and profit. Once this data was obtained the team ran a series of scatter diagrams to determine if there was any correlation between the variables. The following scatter diagrams clearly show a strong correlation between profit and a couple other variables.

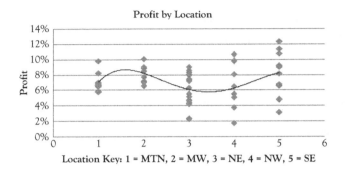

Location Key: 1 = MTN, 2 = MW, 3 = NE, 4 = NW, 5 = SE

The profit by location scatter diagram shows a slight increase in profit for the accounts in the Midwest. The team speculated that this may be the case as rapid line is in the Midwest and has stronger relationships with more local clients. This prompted the team to discuss the structure of the organization including sales reps and direct sale people in the field. The structure was felt by the team to be outside of their scope, so they made a future idea note, and moved on to the following profit by ordering method scatter diagram.

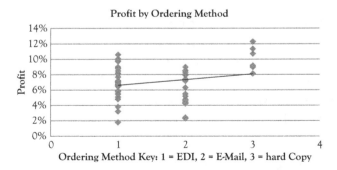

Ordering Method Key: 1 = EDI, 2 = E-Mail, 3 = hard Copy

The team felt that the majority of their largest customers had electronic data exchange (EDI) technology, and that many of their smaller customers did not. The team wasn't sure if this was a direct correlation (cause and effect) or not, but the scatter diagram seemed to show that they were able to make an average profit of ~10 percent with EDI customers, ~6 percent with e-mail customers, and ~6.5 percent with hard-copy accounts. The team concluded that the customers and Rapid Line were better of using EDI methods to eliminate potential wastes.

The team moved on to review the profit by special requirements scatter diagram shown in the following. The team drew no specific conclusion from this plot. It seemed that a typical profit around 8 percent could be achieved with customers with all ranges of special requirements. The key was to serve the customer. As Bill like to say, "The customer may not always be right, but they are always the customer!"

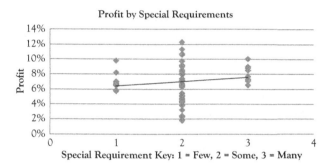

Moving on to the profit by sales scatter diagram; the team observed that the plot almost looks like a histogram turned on its side. They did, however, conclude that their seemed to be more profit potential with smaller customers. Even though the average profits of smaller customers may be similar to average profits of larger customers, some small customer profit exceeded 11 percent. There was, however, risk in pursuing smaller customers in that some smaller customer profits turned out to be very low. The team agreed that smaller accounts were definitely worth pursuing, as long as Rapid Products could protect themselves on the bottom end of profits with perhaps a new pricing model. The team also recommended that the sales team review all smaller accounts with profits less than 6 percent for price increases.

The team too examined the one $1,000,000 account with a profit percent only around 2 percent, for reasons of assignable cause for low profits. The team found assignable cause in last year's numbers in the fact of a large return for defective motors.

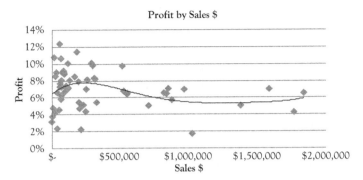

With the correlations shown, the team determined that to maximize profit Rapid Products should target customers with the following attributes:

- Sales volume <$500,000
- In the Midwest
- EDI ordering methods

Also, Rapid Products should review all smaller accounts with profits less than 6 percent for price increases.

The team determined that the scatter diagram analysis should be conducted on an annual basis during the strategic planning process, and adjustments made accordingly with regard to target markets or customers, or products.

Also with the data, the team determined that certain customers pricing should be addressed. Some customers were clearly out of line with pricing norms, and the organization was losing money. The analytical review account-by-account was built into the sales team's semiannual standard work. By conducting the review semiannually, the team believed that they could have an overall positive impact on organization profitability. Standard work documents with step-by-step procedures were drafted and appropriate training provided to the sales teams.

The measurable results from the first review and adjustments yielded an overall profit improvement of 2.5 percent for the customers impacted. The results summary is shown as follows.

	Before initiative	After initiative
Profit % per new account	15.6%	20.5%
New customers per sales resource	5 per $100K	7 per $100K
Profitability by account/customer average	18.9%	23.9%

This effort alone would have a significant overall impact on the organizations' bottom line. The team celebrated their success by attending an afternoon game of the local minor league baseball team.

•••

Jason and Pat's team worked will Bill at the kick-off session and felt strongly that the current CRM system worked well when it was used; however, the problem is that people use it inconsistently, and sporadically. To address this, the team focused around standardized requirements and a simple and effective accountability system. The team developed the following A3 for the engaging new customer processes. Their draft A3 is shown later.

Engaging Potential New Customers Improvement A3 Outline

Problem or Opportunity Statement

The opportunity to address is to apply Lean Six Sigma methods and tools to our engaging potential new customers processes to eliminate waste and improve flow. To simplify, make uniform, and get better results.

Objective and Scope

The scope of this work is the engaging potential new customer processes. The objective is to apply Lean Six Sigma methods and tools to this area to eliminate waste and improve flow of engaging new customers, as well as supporting our overall sales growth rate and profit. The bottom line is we want to grow engage our potential new customers faster and with greater effectiveness.

Current State

A CRM procedure and detailed requirements exists, but is not being followed.

Ideas and Opportunities

- Improving the consistency and standards for data entry into the CRM system.
- Standard work for CRM data entry and accountability. We need to do problem solving to determine why people are not using the system as it is designed, and improve the process with accountability.

Future State

The team envisioned and documented a proposed future state where standard work was followed, and sales people were held accountable for getting the correct information into the CRM system when it was required.

Future Ideas and Opportunities

None identified.

Action Plan and Timeline

The action items were to conduct brief interviews with the sales team members to determine why they were not using the current process or system, and the next session was schedule for 2 weeks out.

Key Measures of Success

The team felt that they had to trust that if they were able to get better use out of the CRM, that the sales team would be able to improve their development of new customers. The metric they focused on to support the Macro Sales A3 metrics are as follows.

1. Percent CRM completion 30, 60, and 90 days after initial customer contact.

Initiative Actions and Outcomes

Since the CRM procedure and detailed requirements exists, but is not being followed, the team initially thought that this may be a simple performance management issue, where people needed to be held accountable for their actions, or in this case, inaction.

However, the team decided to use some basic problem-solving techniques to see if they could determine why the sales people were not using the system. Their initial findings after interviews and focus group sessions with key sales team members, was that the system requirements specified too many details even before the potential customer became a customer, and then, once the potential customer became a customer, the focus was on delivering the first products versus completing the CRM data management requirements.

The team felt that they needed to listen and respond to the issues the sales people brought to their attention. To do this the team went through an item by item review of the CRM data requirements as well as the timing regarding when the information was required. The team split the data requirements into the categories of (1) mandatory or value added, (2) desired, and (3) nonvalue added. The nonvalue-added items were removed from the work instructions in effort to streamline the process. An example of this work is shown in the following.

	1	2	3
CRM Item	**VA**	**Desired**	**NVA**
Customer information			
Name	X		
Address(s)	X		
Sales		X	
Employment			X
Union or non-union			X
Their customer names		X	
Primary language			X
Advertisement media			X
•			
•			

(continued)

(Continued)

CRM Item	1 VA	2 Desired	3 NVA
•			
Contact(s) information			
Name	X		
Phone number	X		
E-mail address	X		
Supervisor or manager		X	
Key employees in group		X	
Family names			
Birthday			X
Favorite sports teams			X
Favorite pass time or hobbies			X
•			
•			
•			

After the CRM data requirements were streamlined, the improvement team developed an interactive training session that would outline the new simplified requirements to the sales team, and was valuable, that they would be more apt to complete the requirements as specified.

The improvement team also met with Bill, and indicated to him that he played a critical part in holding the sales people accountable to complete this valuable data entry. Bill agreed to support the improvements and hold the sales team accountable by reviewing a CRM completion log on a weekly basis. This review process would be built into Bill's standard work.

The measurable results from the first review and adjustments yielded an overall profit improvement of 2.5 percent for the customers impacted. The results summary is shown in the following.

Percent CRM completion after	30 days	60 days	90 days
Before initiative	22%	43%	65%
Six months after initiative	68%	93%	99%

This effort would have a significant impact for the sales team and the organization as they quickly learned that if they completed the CRM requirements on time, they had less questions and e-mails to deal with as the customer was brought on board. The sales team felt that they were gaining extra time, by not having to address all the questions, and the inside sales teams were happy in that they had the information they needed, and could do their work without constantly bothering the sales person. This effort was truly a win-win-win for the customer, the sales people, and the inside sales people. The CRM software supplier actually asked Bill if they could use him in a website success story!

•••

Mary and Sandy's team worked with Bill in their kick-off session and developed the following A3 outline.

Developing a Trusting Relationship Improvement A3 Outline

Problem or Opportunity Statement

The opportunity to address is to apply Lean Six Sigma methods and tools to our developing trusting relationship processes to eliminate waste and improve flow. To simplify, make uniform, and get better results.

Objective and Scope

The scope of this work is the developing trusting relationships processes. The objective is to apply Lean Six Sigma methods and tools to this area to eliminate waste and improve flow of developing trusting relationships with potential new customers, as well as to support our overall sales growth rate and profit. The bottom line is we want to develop trusting relationships faster and more effectively in effort to bring new customers and sales on faster.

Current State

Currently, everyone develops trusting relationships in their own way. Some are better at it than others based on their consistent results. We want to learn from our high performers, and teach our entire sales team improved methods in effort to achieve improvements.

Ideas and Opportunities

- BPs and standardized work methods. Standard work around BPs.
- Counselor selling.

Future State

The intent is to have a solid training program for our sales force, which includes standard BPs, where results can be measured.

Future Ideas and Opportunities

None identified.

Action Plan and Timeline

The team agreed to allow Mary and Sandy to get the performance data needed to determine BPs. Other team members agreed to research the latest in sales training programs for future discussions. After the high performers are identified, interviews with the top five high performers will be conducted to determine if there are any common BPs. Finally, the team plans to develop an in-house training program for new and existing sales people. The entire timeline will take ~6 months to complete.

Key Measures of Success

The team felt that the macro sales metrics also did a fine job in measuring their performance. The team believed that if the sales BP training program worked, each of the following key success measures would show the cause and effect impact:

1. New sales $ per sales resource $
2. New customers per sales resource $
3. New sales $ with existing customers per sales resource $

The team also considered a customer survey instrument to determine how sales people are developing trusting relationships, but chose to deal with this at a different time.

Initiative Actions and Outcomes

The teams worked to design and execute a brief voice of the customer (VOC) survey instrument where customers score their relationship with Rapid Products personnel. Once the survey data was collected and analyzed, the team would identify BPs.

The team also completed a study and analysis of sales training programs. The team took the best they could find in their search, and combined it with their own thoughts regarding sales training, and developed a Rapid Products Sales Training Program. This took several months, but the training also covered the CRM system, as well as soft selling skills.

The VOC data clearly showed that one group of customers had a significantly higher than average scores for relationships, so the team conducted deeper study of the tools and techniques used by the lead sales person for this area.

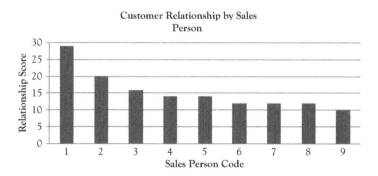

Customer Relationship by Sales Person

The team found that Eric, coded as number 1 in the previous graph, used certain techniques consistently with his clients. He had developed a series of questions that he would use to introduce himself and Rapid Products to the potential new client. Once the potential client became a customer, Eric had developed a standard method and frequency to follow-up with every customer. The team asked Eric if they could use his methods and questions to develop a BP method for the entire sales team. Eric enthusiastically agreed, and wanted to help the team. They immediately added Eric to the subteam, and began developing the new BPs. Eric had developed for his personal use, new and existing customer guidelines and standard questions that he would use to manage his customer relationships. The team used these guidelines and questions to develop standard work BPs, and incorporated these into the new sales training program.

It took a while until the team felt that the impact of their work would impact the macro key success measures, and they were right. In fact, it was hard to draw a direct correlation between their work and the macro sales metrics, so they added a VOC metric which they believed would be a better measure the impact of their work. They used the initial VOC survey data as a baseline, and after six months completed another survey. The team developed a once-per-year plan to administer the VOC survey, but was pleased with their results after the first six months of work.

The measurable results from the first review and adjustments yielded an overall profit improvement of 2.5 percent for the customers impacted. The results summary is shown in the following.

	Baseline VOC	After initiative VOC
Voice of the customer results	82.6%	96.8%

•••

Jack and Julie's team had requested an extra week to get their A3 drafted, but they found that once they scheduled the kick-off work session, things went faster than they thought, and the team was more enthusiastic than Jack thought that they might be. The team members actually were glad that some of these issues were finally being addressed. Jack and Julie's team developed the following A3 with Bill's guidance.

Develop Need and Advocate Solutions Improvement A3 Outline

Problem or Opportunity Statement

The opportunity to address is to apply Lean Six Sigma methods and tools to our developing need and advocating solutions processes to eliminate waste and improve flow, and to simplify, make uniform, and get better results.

Objective and Scope

The scope of this work is the developing need and advocating solutions processes. The objective is to apply Lean Six Sigma methods and tools to this area to eliminate waste and improve flow of bringing solutions to our customers, as well as supporting our overall sales growth rate and profit. The bottom line is we want to develop and get solutions to our customers faster and more effectively, while becoming more profitable.

Current State

The team mapped out the RFP process. The CS was fraught with problems, and the map and the issues log showed this.

The RFP process was confusing and cumbersome. Each sales person wanted things their own way in effort to meet their customer's needs and desires. The people working in the RFP process were constantly re-doing and fixing proposals for resubmission. It seemed there were no standards in how the RFP's were processes, and no standards with the information required to initiate an RFP.

Another issue was after they actually won a new contract; it seemed that the proposal agreements did not typically match the original proposal. This created more confusion and wasted a great deal of time and effort in having to sort things out to determine what would actually be supplied and at what cost. Often what was agreed to, was not properly quoted and the organization found they absorbed losses rather than dealing with issues up front.

The team prioritized their opportunities and continued to work.

Ideas and Opportunities

- RFP process speed. RFP standard work, information, and processing improvements
- FTT quality improvement by requiring specific information upfront.

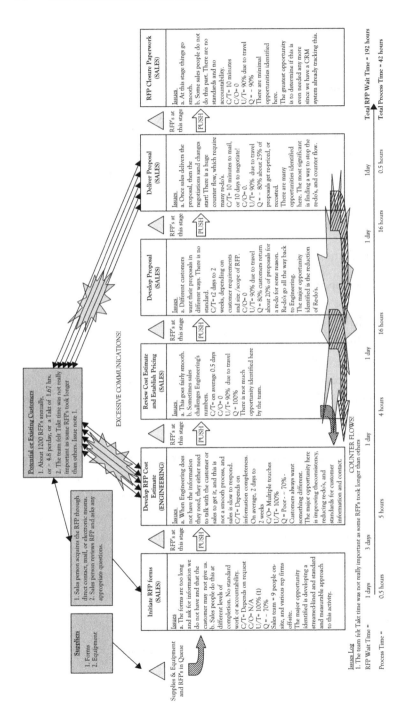

Request For Proposal (RFP) CSM

Future State

The basic idea for the future state is that RFPs would come in with the required information the first time, and accurate proposals would be developed and delivered to potential customers with fewer need for revisions and adjustments.

Future Ideas and Opportunities

None identified.

Action Plan and Timeline

The team began discussing what information was needed to complete an RFP properly, and felt that they should establish a separate work session to detail these requirements. The direction was to develop a standardized RFP form that would be completed by the sales person to initiate an RFP. The organization already had a basic form, yet it has been historically incomplete when previously submitted. The team indicated to Bill that he may have to use his authority to enforce the new methods, and Bill assured the team that they had his full support.

The team also agreed that they had to start tracking key data such as the number of proposals that had to be revised because the information was not correct in the initial RFP. A subteam agreed to develop and implement a log sheet to track inappropriate RFP reworks.

The team scheduled a weekly work session to complete this work. They felt that they should be able to have a draft of new process in 6 weeks.

Key Measures of Success

The key success measure for this team is the number of inappropriate RFP reworks or revisions per month. The team believed that if inappropriate RFP reworks were reduced, the macro sales process key success measures would improve as fewer resources would be used to complete RFPs or more RFPs could be completed by the current resources.

Macro Sale Process Success Metrics:

1. New sales $ per sales resource $
2. New customers per sales resource $
3. New sales $ with existing customers per sales resource $

Initiative Actions and Outcomes

The team continued to meet weekly and more deeply developed the current and future state maps. The future state map is shown later, and it identifies a greatly improved process, with colocated teams, and a weekly work session to speed the RFP process, and reduce re-do's.

The significant improvement action items implemented over a four-month period are as follows.

Jack and Julie's team improvements over a four-month period:

1. Streamlined RFP form to require only the most critical, value added data. More detailed data will be acquired if needed at the team session, or before if the proposal is needed sooner.
2. An RFP team will be developed and will colocate in a common and open office arrangement, and cross-train in various roles.
3. The RFP team will develop and follow standard work for the RFP process and weekly work session.
4. The weekly RFP session will be used to clarify all data needs and build flow and teamwork.
5. The weekly joint session will clarify all issues and set the action plan for key action items.
6. Standard RFP format is in development, but we must meet the customers' needs as a priority. This may mean we cannot standardize our RFP proposal format completely.
7. Improved up-front data acquisition in the weekly work sessions, should reduce back-end re-do's.
8. The team eliminated the sales follow-up process entirely, as this will be tracked in the weekly RFP work session.

Implementing these improvement items took time and teamwork. The team realized the improvements and felt the impact almost immediately.

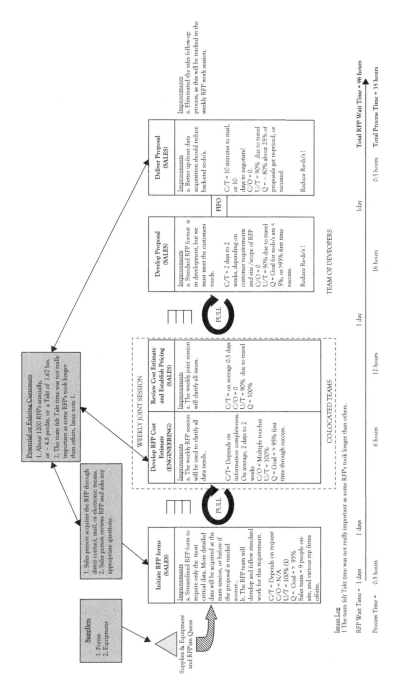

Request For Proposal (RFP) FSM

Their key success measure is the number of inappropriate re-do's or corrections to the RFP cost estimate or actual proposals. Once the team had the systems in place and running, the number of inappropriate re-do's dropped dramatically. The results summary is shown in the following.

	Before initiative	After initiative
Time to complete a RFP	192 hours	96 hours (50% improvement)
Time to process a RFP	42 hours	35 hours (17% improvement)
Number of inappropriate Re-do's	30%	<10%*

(*The re-do improvement alone saved over 10,000 hours or $100,000 annually!)

The results of these improvements allowed Rapid Products to improve the speed of the RFP proposal process, as well as complete 17 percent more RFPs with the same staff.

•••

With Bill's guidance during the kick-off session, Amy and Tom's team developed the following A3 for the customer support team.

Supporting Direction and Decision Improvement A3 Outline

Problem or Opportunity Statement

The opportunity to address is to apply Lean Six Sigma methods and tools to our supporting direction and decision processes to eliminate waste and improve flow, to simplify, make uniform, and get better results.

Objective and Scope

The scope of this work is the supporting direction and decision processes. The objective is to apply Lean Six Sigma methods and tools to this area to eliminate waste and improve flow of serving our customers, as well as supporting our overall sales growth rate and profit. The bottom line is we want to improve and streamline our customer service processes with the same (or fewer) sales resources.

Current State

The team mapped out the customer on-boarding process, and learned that there were several key improvement opportunities.

The biggest problem with the CS was reconciling the proposal with the actual agreement, and getting the proper customer information uploaded into the system. The cause of these issues is believed to be the poor performance with the CRM system, and multiple proposals developed during the RFP process. The team felt that as the other areas made improvements the on-boarding process would improve as well.

Ideas and Opportunities

Improve the new customer on-boarding process. This process overlaps or links to the RFP process.

Future State

Instead of the customer service people dreading the on-boarding process, and the new customer becoming frustrated with multiple questions that they may feel they've answered before; the future state is envisioned to be a smooth and pleasant process for the customer and the internal customer service and support people.

Future Ideas and Opportunities

An idea did come up during the team's kick-off session that the entire process needs to be aligned and tied together, and that perhaps different organization of sales teams may help.

Action Plan and Timeline

To help facilitate the customer on-boarding process the team's primary objective is to document the required information for properly on-boarding new customers. The team began to do this during the kick-off session, but ran out of time and scheduled another session. The team believed that their end product would be a detailed checklist to be followed by the sales team when they land a new customer. This and appropriate training on the requirements were worked into a 12-week work plan.

The team also designed into their work plan the development of survey instrument to capture the impression of the customer through the on-boarding process.

Key Measures of Success

The key success measure for the on-boarding improvement team is the impression of the customer regarding how smoothly the process goes. To capture this measure, the team will develop a survey instrument, and establish a baseline data point for reference and improvement tracking.

The team believes that if they can improve the overall impression of a new customer through the on-boarding process, that the organization may gain more business, and have a positive impact on the macro sales process metrics of:

1. New sales $ per sales resource $
2. New customers per sales resource $
3. New sales $ with existing customers per sales resource $

Initiative Actions and Outcomes

The team continued to meet weekly over the next couple of months. Through the development of the CS map shown later, the team clearly identified the major improvement opportunity of improving the CRM data entry on customer on-boarding. Through the monthly team sessions Bill was conducting the team and knew that this topic was also being addressed by Jack and Julie's team. Amy and Tom set up a couple work sessions with Jack and Julie to ensure that these areas were being addressed appropriately.

With this work on track, the team looked at their next biggest opportunities which were the conflicts between the proposal terms and features,

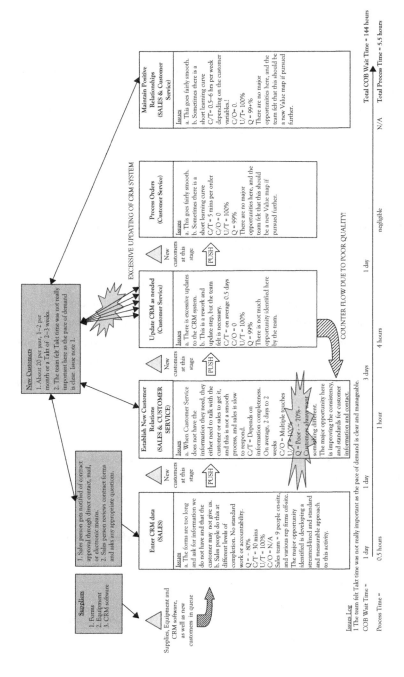

Customer On-Boarding (COB) CSM

and the actual requirements from the customer. These conflicts ranged from invoice dates, advance shipping notices, special packaging requirements, and similar items. Seen as "trivial" by the sales team, these issues cost Rapid Products profit and time to manage in customer service. Some issues even required requoting to the customer. When this happened, sales was reluctant to approach the customer with price increases that should have been caught in the proposal process, and the customer reaction when this occurred was potentially disastrous.

The team knew that the information gathering in the RFP process was being worked on as well by Jack and Julie's team, but in effort to address the customer on-boarding process, the team began to develop a standard checklist to discuss with the new customer on the initial introductory conversation. The team positioned this with the customer as a BP in customer service. Sales would explain that there is a customer on-boarding process designed to acquaint the customer to our customer service team, as well as to close any open issues as we start our business relationship. The team believed that a stand checklist and process for customer on-boarding would reduce the counter flow and rework in their area.

The team also knew through discussions with Bill, that Sandy and Mary's team was implementing a VOC survey process. The team worked with Sandy and Mary's team to include questions about the on-boarding process in their survey. With this data the team could show the impact of their improvements.

After the implementation of the customer on-boarding process improvements the team was able to reduce the stress and frustration of the customer service representatives as well as the customers in measurable ways. The results from their work are shown later.

	Baseline VOC	After initiative VOC
Voice of the customer		
On-boarding question results	89.6%	98%

	Before initiative	After initiative
Rework hours per COB process	4 hours	<1 hour (>75% improvement)
Employee stress with COB process	Yes	Reduced
Customer stress with COB process	Yes	Reduced

An additional benefit that is not measured is that the sales team can now promote a BP customer on-boarding process to help gain business.

•••

Macro Process Results Summary

Over the four-month period that the improvement teams worked on their individual projects, Bill continued to document and summarizes the team results. Bill had learned from Sam that a critical point was that each of the team's individual results all supported and added up to overall organization success. The macro results are summarized by bill in the following table.

Identifying potential clients and customers—co-leaders: Tammy and Deb		
	Before initiative	After initiative
Profit % per new account	15.6%	20.5%
New customers per sales resource	5 per $100,000	7 per $100,000
Profitability by account/customer average	18.9%	23.9%

Engaging potential new customers—co-leaders; Jason and Pat			
Percent CRM completion after	30 days	60 days	90 days
Before initiative	22%	43%	65%
6 months after initiative	68%	93%	99%

Developing a trusting relationship—co-leaders: Mary and Sandy		
	Baseline VOC	After initiative VOC
Voice of the customer results	82.6%	96.8%

Develop need and advocate solutions—co-leaders: Jack and Julie		
	Before initiative	After initiative
Time to complete a RFP	192 hours	96 hours (50% improvement)
Time to process a RFP	42 hours	35 hours (17% improvement)
Number of inappropriate re-do's	30%	<10%*

(*The re-do improvement alone saved over 10,000 hours or $100,000 annually!)

Supporting direction and decision—co-leaders: Amy and Tom		
	Baseline VOC	After initiative VOC
Voice of the customer		
On-boarding question results	89.6%	98%
	Before initiative	After initiative
Rework hours per COB process	4 hours	<1 hour (>75% improvement)
Employee stress with COB process	Yes	Reduced
Customer stress with COB process	Yes	Reduced

An additional benefit that is not measured is that the sales team can now promote a BP customer on-boarding process to help gain business.

Macro Key Measures of Success:

	Before initiative	After initiative
New sales $ per sales resource $	73:1	119:1 (63% increase)
New customers per sales resource $	20	35 (75% increase)
New sales $ with existing customers per sales resource $	12:1	>22:1 (87% increase)

When Bill completed his summary report, he could hardly believe his eyes. The stories about how Lean Sigma could impact an organization were not just stories, but real possibilities, and Bill's teams had been able to achieve the order of magnitude results in a very short period of time. Bill's excitement got the best of him, and he printed the summary report and ran off to talk to Sam.

"Sam, Sam!" Bill yelled and waved as he saw Sam walking into his office. Bill followed Sam into his office, and slid the results summary report over to Sam, and said, "Take a look at these numbers." But before he gave Sam a chance to look he started talking.

"I can't believe it, but you were right, Lean Sigma has had a huge positive impact in my sales area. I guess it does apply to sales process, and it's not as magical as I thought!"

"I never had a doubt Bill," replied Sam. "It's been working for my suppliers' sales processes for some time now."

Bill grabbed the report from Sam's hand and said, "I'm going to get this into the company newsletter. I've got to go. I'll see you later, oh yea, thanks for your help Sam."

Sam sat there for a minute dumbfounded, but smiling; reflecting on the reaction Bill had to the latest reports, and then got back to work.

Discussion Questions

1. Critically evaluate the standard agenda and the training notes that were mailed to the participants prior to the meeting. Do you see a value in using the work session record template in the related meetings you organize? Why or Why not? Explain.

2. Do you have experience with process improvement A3 forms? Do you think it is a useful tool? How can your organization make use of this tool?

3. Critically evaluate the macro sales process A3 form completed by Bill. What do you like the most and what are some things you would do differently?

4. Critically evaluate the A3 process and form prepared by Tammy and Deb's group for identifying potential new client processes. What do you like the most and what are some things you would do differently?

5. Critically evaluate the A3 process and form prepared by Jason and Pat's group for engaging potential new customers processes. What do you like the most and what are some things you would do differently?

6. Critically evaluate the A3 process and form prepared by Mary and Sandy's group for developing a trusting relationship process. What do you like the most and what are some things you would do differently?

7. Critically evaluate the A3 process and form prepared by Jack and Julie's team for developing and advocating solutions processes. What do you like the most and what are some things you would do differently?

8. Critically evaluate the A3 process and form prepared by Amy and Tom's team for supporting direction and design improvement processes. What do you like the most and what are some things you would do differently?

9. What lessons can we learn from these different A3 applications? How do you ensure that they are done right and add value?

CHAPTER 8

Making Sales Cultural Transitions

Bill and his sales team had made great progress. There had been many ups and downs during the improvement initiatives, but overall the teams were really making a positive impact. The teams were getting good at identifying current state data, developing process flow, and value stream maps, and then creating future state plan, do check, act (PDCA) experiments to try to make improvements. However, there were still some areas that Bill was wondering about. For example, Bill was concerned about the people side of the improvement initiatives. Some of the people-side issues Bill was concerned about were training to sustain the gains and momentum, the discipline to stick to the standard work, and the accountability. Managing sales people had sometimes been compared to herding cats!

In the early days of the transformation Sam had Bill work with his people to develop a current state culture assessment. To do this Bill lead a brainstorming session with his sales team, and developed the following current state culture diagram.

This map is in a cause and effect format, and it shows clearly the problems and potential target improvement areas. Teams can use this or similar methods to document their current culture and target areas for improvement. With this completed, Bill thought it would be a good idea to lead the sales team through the future state culture development to show what they wanted to become. They called this the future state culture, and used it as a vision for them to achieve through the continuous improvement efforts. The following future state culture map was developed by Bill's sales team. They all agreed to try to live up to the vision. The implementation of the improvement teams went a long way toward helping the teams achieve the future state culture.

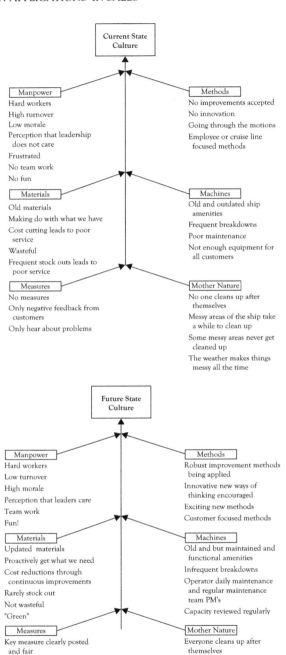

Sam had assisted Bill with this current state to future state culture mapping process to help Bill's sales team understand where they were going and what they were trying to become with the Lean Sigma improvement methods.

Sam was most impressed with some of the sales training that Bill had developed, and thought he might be able to use it in the supply chain area. "So Bill, tell me about your sales training program, your people are clearly doing something different than my folks are with the supply chain. Your people are constantly interacting with customers, and I can tell they've had some specific training regarding how to talk and listen to customers, so what is it?" Sam asked Bill.

Bill said, "Let's go talk with our HR manager, Ann, she's the one who developed the program." The two took a walk to the HR offices to meet with Ann.

At the HR offices Ann outlined their customer service and sales training programs. Ann explained, "I've studied the Disney training programs and had the opportunity to attend several courses at the highly regarded Disney Institute. The Disney Institute is widely recognized as a world leader in service training and development. I'm taking a page from the Walt Disney Company where they call all of their employee's *cast members*. A cast member has a different meaning than an employee. A cast member has to be able to play a role. The cast member's role may be a sales person or customer service person. In any case, a cast member is expected to act in an appropriate way, to play their role as though they are at the happiest place on earth!"

Ann continued, "We are trying to instill this philosophy at Rapid Products. To do this, I use six key training classes. Every new sales or customer service employee receives the following courses over their first three months of being hired." Our programs are as follows:

Basic Training Programs

- Orientation
- *Lean Sigma Basics*: Ptacek and Motwani.
- *The Seven Habits of Highly Effective People*: Steven Covey.
- *Developing Customer Loyalty*: Jeffrey Gitomer.

- *FISH! Philosophy*: Stephen C. Lundin, PhD, Harry Paul, John Christensen.
- Counselor selling

The orientation was not unlike any organization's orientation training. This course introduced the new employees to the organization and covered the following topics.

 a. General orientation and facts about the cruise line

 b. Vision, mission, and values

 c. Organization structure

 d. Key performance indicators (KPIs)

 e. Performance expectations

 f. Safety rules

"Since the organization was making so much progress with the Lean Sigma methods and tools, we recently updated the key training programs to include the basics of Lean Sigma. Now the new employees knew what was expected of them regarding continuous improvement, and how they could participate. I recruit various area leaders to facilitate this training," continued Ann.

The seven habits training covered the following seven habits from the popular book by Steven Covey.

 1. Be proactive

 2. Begin with the end in mind

 3. Put first things first

 4. Think win-win

 5. Seek first to understand, then to be understood

 6. Synergize

 7. Sharpen the saw (continue learning and teaching)

The objective of this training was to help people develop a success habit for their personal and professional lives. These habits were described as *expected behaviors* of employees and were reviewed during their performance appraisals.

The developing customer loyalty training was used to help employees more effectively help internal and external customers no matter what the need. This training taught specific skills, tools, and techniques. Practice time was provided in class so people could develop their skills. One of the key concepts taught was that we want loyal customers who come back time and time again, and refer our cruise line to other people. One critical technique taught in class is the 3 Rs +1. This technique teaches cast members how to respond to customers who need help. When a customer asks for assistance, employees are expected to do the following;

- *React* to the situation and customer emotion with certain phrases in a sincere manner.
- *Respond* to the need in an appropriate manner to develop customer loyalty as they would want it responded to.
- *Resolve* the issue to the customers satisfaction: How they would want the situation resolved it if they were the customer.
- *1* Do one extra thing for the customer that is not expected, but welcomed.

"This is a simple and powerful technique if done properly," Ann continued.

"We use the FISH! Philosophy video, which highlights the operations and philosophy of the Pike's Fish Market in Seattle, Washington, to instill a sense of service and fun in each employee. The video illustrates the power of four simple principles of customer service and dealing with people." The FISH philosophies are as follows:

1. Play
2. Be there
3. Make their day
4. Choose your attitude

The "play" principle shows people how to make work fun for the customer and the worker. Several specific methods are developed during the training. The "be there" principle helps employees connect with customers and people in a more meaningful way. It helps people be more sincere in their efforts to help people. "Make their day" helps people to understand what it takes to develop customer loyalty, and is complimentary of the customer loyalty training. It gives everyone additional ideas on how to develop customer loyalty and future referrals. Finally, the "choose your attitude" training delivers the message that she expects every employee to be the best every day, and only they can choose their attitude. This fits well with the "Seven Habits" training on being proactive, as well as many other habits.

The counselor selling program is where we teach our sales people to be counselors to our customers, not just sales people. Their goal is to solve problems for our customers whether it is our service or not that is the solution. If customers see our sales people keeping their best interest in mind, they will call us time and time again to allow us to help solve their problems. It is our hope that eventually our services will develop to serve their needs. At a minimum, customers will develop a high level of trust and team work with Rapid Products.

"The training doesn't stop there." Ann explained, "Every employee continues to receive refresher training on these topics on a regular basis. This supports the culture future state targets. It all fits together, and we're making such huge improvements in retention and customer feedback."

After listening to Ann's passion about this training, Sam asked Bill and Ann if they would consider delivering some of this training to his supply chain team. After the help Sam had provided to Bill and the slumping sales team, Bill quickly agreed to help Sam, and the two began developing the cross-organizational training plan.

Discussion Questions

1. What do you think of Bill's concerns regarding the people side of the improvement initiatives? Do you encounter the same concerns in your organization? How does your organization and you deal with them?

2. What do you think of the process used by Bill to address these concerns? Do you think it was a good idea to do a current state and future state cultural assessment? Why or why not? What lessons can your organization learn from this process?

3. Critically evaluate the sales, customer service, and loyalty training programs that Bill and Ann have developed. Do you think these programs are appropriate?

CHAPTER 9

Achieving, Sustaining, and Celebrating Sales Success

Bill had been working on the Lean Sigma improvements for nearly two years, and was invited to Rapid Products's annual Supplier Day to present his success story. During a break in the sessions, Ray caught up to Bill and asked the following.

"We've been doing this Lean Sigma thing for nearly six years now and have made some great progress. We are actually growing now, and becoming quite profitable. But the teams are losing their enthusiasm and the whole thing is starting to seem stale. Any hints on how to re-energize the teams?" asked Ray.

"We always go back to the basics to recharge our teams. It's important to show your commitment. Remember the key enablers? Ask yourself what, if anything is missing?" Bill replied.

Key Enablers for Lean Sigma Success:

1. Leadership establishing, communicating, and living up to the vision, mission, and values
2. Resource commitment
3. Training and education
4. Process and results focused
5. Policy deployment and goal alignment
6. Total system or value stream focus
7. Employee involvement
8. Perseverance and commitment

Source: Lean Thinking and PPS.

Bill continued, "We also try to come up with some new challenges or themes to keep things fresh. One time when we set new goals for sales, everyone cried that 'We can't get any more work with the economy in a dead fall!' So we told the teams that when we meet the new goals, we would celebrate by having the management team wash their cars. The winning team would get free car washes for a year. This really got the teams fired-up, and we had a lot of fun with the challenge. In fact, when the managers were washing cars, a local newspaper reported on it, and everyone enjoyed seeing an article about how fun it is to work at Rapid Products. Our customers also took note as well. That was quite a fun celebration."

"We then created another theme to push accomplishment even farther. We created a competition within the organization, and the winning team with the most improvements would get a free vacation day. Again we had a lot of fun with this. It took about a year to achieve the goal, but we succeeded in raising the bar of achievement. You might try a theme or a challenge, or internal competition to get some excitement back into the improvement effort," explained Bill.

"When you're managing change in an organization, things can get difficult," continued Bill. Bill sketched the following illustration on the white board, and explained. "You see, at first, once everyone sees that you're serious about improving, and gets over the shock and denial, people begin to see how the Lean Sigma improvements can help them. They start to see some quick hitting improvements, and are optimistic. Then, when the 'low hanging fruit' or easy projects have been implemented, things get tougher, and improvements are harder to find. When this happens, things start to plateau or level out. If left alone, this plateau will turn into pessimism and doubt. At this point people need to see management's commitment to Lean Sigma methods and tools. Too many leaders throw in the towel at this point, and say Lean Sigma doesn't work.

If managers and leaders redouble their efforts and commitments at this point, things will start to turn around, and many more significant gains will occur. The key is to push through the trough or 'organizational stress' as quickly as possible, by sticking to key projects and the Lean Sigma methods and tools."

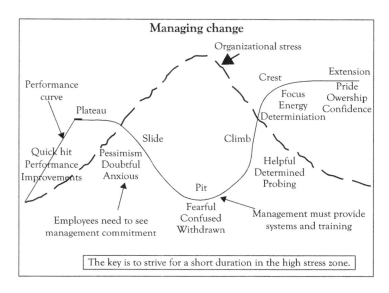

Ray said, "That's interesting, but I think we are beyond that now, and I just want to get some more excitement around the pigments plus. I think a challenge—something big, will be a good way to get the excitement back."

"In Jim Collins's book *Good to Great*, he called them *Big Hairy Audacious Goals* (BHAGs), and many organizations have them. They provide long-term focus and can be fun," Bill added.

"Another key is to continue to hold people accountable to use the Lean Sigma methods and tools. This should be built right into your performance management system. Keep to the accountability sessions or *Meeting Rhythms* as Harnish called them in his book *Mastering the Rockefeller Habits*. In the book, Harnish describes a meeting rhythm with daily huddles, weekly, monthly, and quarterly work sessions to review progress to goals, ensure resources are provided, and to hold people and teams accountable for results. This is a key to sustaining the effort. Make these regular work sessions have standard work for you and your area leaders. Perform layered process audits to make sure they are doing them, and doing them correctly. This will let the teams see that these are important to you, and to their success," Bill added.

"Boy, sustaining the effort is hard work!" replied Ray "and you've really become quite the expert. Nice work Bill, and thanks for your help," Ray concluded.

"Well Ray, you helped me when I needed it, and as you know, and Lean Sigma philosophy is to share the knowledge. It's the least I could do."

Discussion Questions

1. What do you think of Bill's statement that "We always go back to the basics to recharge our team?" Why do you think it is important to go back to the basics and to remember the key enablers?

2. Do you agree with Bill that, "We also try to come up with some new challenges or themes to keep things fresh." What does your organization do in this area?

3. Why is it critical for an organization to hold people accountable to use the Lean Sigma methods and tools? What does your organization do to make their people accountable?

Suggestions for Further Reading

Possible books that are related to the themes covered by this book:

- Sales and Marketing the Six Sigma Way [Paperback] Michael Webb, and Tom Gorman, 2010 Sales Performance Consultants Inc., ISBN 9780615751887.
- *Coaching Salespeople into Sales Champions: A Tactical Playbook for Managers and Executives* [Hardcover] Keith Rosen arch 14, 2008| ISBN-10: 0470142510, | ISBN-13: 978-0470142516.
- *Introduction to Sales Process Improvement: Gaining More of the Right Customers at Higher Margins and Lower Costs with Lean and Six Sigma* [Paperback] Michael Webb 2010 Sales Performance Consultants Inc., ISBN 0-9771072-0-5.
- *Sales Process Engineering: A Personal Workshop* [Hardcover] ASQ Quality Press Paul H. Selden November 1996, ISBN-10: 0873894189, ISBN-13: 978-0873894180.

Index

OTHER TITLES IN OUR SELLING AND SALES FORCE MANAGEMENT COLLECTION

Buddy LaForge, University of Louisville and Thomas Ingram, Colorado State University, Collection Editors

- *Sales Technology: Making the Most of Your Investment* by Nikolaos Panagopoulos
- *Effective Sales Force Automation and Customer Relationship Management: A Focus on Selection and Implementation* by Raj Agnihotri and Adam Rapp
- *Customer-Oriented Sales Management Practices: Text and Cases* by Ramendra Singh
- *Sales Force Ethical Decision Making: A Guide for Sales Professionals* by Lawrence Chonko and Fernando Jaramillo
- *Managing and Conducting Sales as a Project: Synergies Between Sales Methodologies and Project Management Techniques* by Richard Owen
- *Competitive Intelligence and the Sales Force: How to Gain Market Leadership Through Competitive Intelligence* by Joël Le Bon

Announcing the Business Expert Press Digital Library

*Concise E-books Business Students Need
for Classroom and Research*

This book can also be purchased in an e-book collection by your library as
- a one-time purchase,
- that is owned forever,
- allows for simultaneous readers,
- has no restrictions on printing, and
- can be downloaded as PDFs from within the library community.

Our digital library collections are a great solution to beat the rising cost of textbooks. E-books can be loaded into their course management systems or onto students' e-book readers.

The **Business Expert Press** digital libraries are very affordable, with no obligation to buy in future years. For more information, please visit **www.businessexpertpress.com/librarians**. To set up a trial in the United States, please email **sales@businessexpertpress.com**.